# LONDON
# THEATRES

# LONDON THEATRES

**MICHAEL COVENEY**

**PETER DAZELEY**

FOREWORD BY **MARK RYLANCE**

FRANCES
LINCOLN

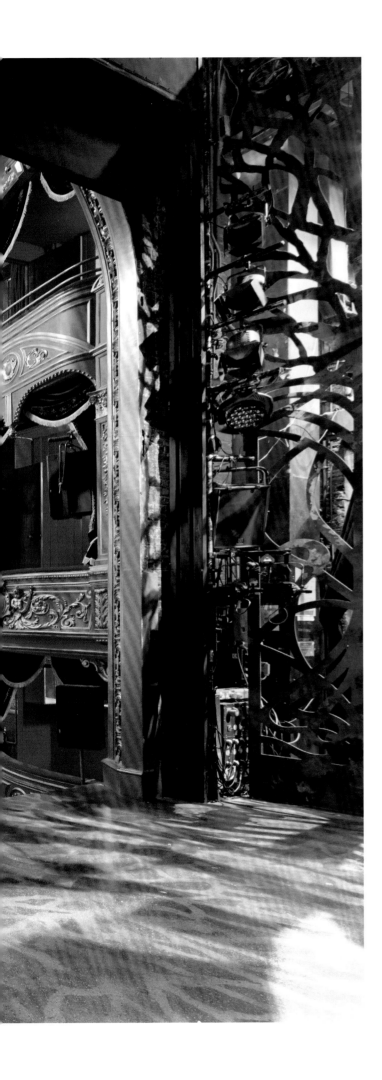

# Contents

HALF TITLE *The Palace Theatre at night.*
TITLE PAGE *Men's quick-change area, Theatre Royal Drury Lane.*
LEFT *View from the back of the stage, Theatre Royal Stratford East.*

# Foreword

## by Mark Rylance

In a theatre you need to hear the truth. In a cinema you need to see it. This is not to say that the visual and auditory experiences aren't an important part of each medium. People don't realize the importance of the wonderful voice in the appeal of a successful film actor like George Clooney because one is so captivated by the expression of thought and emotion in his eyes. But, in a theatre, no one can get as close as a camera, many are more than ten rows away, so the actors' eyes are distant. The thought and emotion need to be heard in the voice. The eyes are important in the theatre but at distance the body even more so. A quiet voice in film and a still body in the theatre are very effective, as they allow the audience to focus on the most powerful storyteller of each discipline. Contrast, focus and contradiction are everything in acting.

Also, when many of the beautiful theatres in this book were built, theatrical lighting was far less powerful than it is today. You will see that most lighting fixtures, sockets, brackets and poles are not part of the original design. Nowadays they often crowd out the all-important private boxes that connect the auditorium with the stage. Footlights and such would have given some visual dominance to the actors, but nothing like the blazing stage we now witness, or darkened auditorium.

Some of these theatres will have employed gaslight, which, I presume, while an audience was present, could only be turned down in the auditorium, never extinguished. Everyone remained visible. Actors used make-up to strengthen their facial expressions, but really until the designer Edward Gordon Craig added a third dimension to scenery, there was only so much an actor could visually do in front of a painted canvas. So we clap our hands and make funny noises when we first walk out onto a stage, any stage, to check the acoustics. I also look up at the ceiling.

In my experience, the best of these old theatres always have some circular device in their ornate ceiling. I once toured *Hamlet* to eleven different cities in Britain, playing all the old theatres: the King's in Glasgow, the Palace in Manchester, the Olympia in Dublin. I learned to look up as soon as I arrived on Monday morning and, when I saw a circular pattern above the auditorium, I knew we would be all right that week. You will see a few in this book. If there wasn't a circle, I knew we would have a difficult time. It wasn't just that the acoustics were probably problematic but it was going to be harder to convince the audience that they were in the same room with us. We would be unconsciously perceived to be masters at the head of the table and they passive diners down the sides. There is no top or bottom to a circular table or room. There is a centre and a circumference. The centre is invisible and the circumference visible though its measurement forever irrational. I love all the theatres in this book, but I feel the greatest theatres always have the irrational curve of a circle in their seating and design. Why?

Most years I go walking in the mountains with my brother and a group of friends. When we light a fire at sunset, we roll rocks around to sit on and intuitively create the earliest storytelling theatre known to man. The centre is where the heat is and that heat spreads fairly to each walker sat round in a circle, as do the stories of the day's sights, the jokes, hopes and remembrances, the songs, and sometimes the dance, more to keep warm, I must confess, than to represent any dying fawn or lovesick swan. There is a shared experience. Someone contributes to the story just as someone contributes logs to the fire. The fire and story both share the centre. Our faces are lit alike by the imagination and the red glow of the flames. I love how many of these theatres choose red for the colour of their seats, as if conscious of their great-grandfather, the primeval fire! Of course they are not theatres in the round, such as Shakespeare's Globe. They are not even the semi-circle of a Greek amphitheatre, such as the Olivier at the National Theatre, but they haven't forgotten their past. Their fire curtains give them away.

I was asked to write something about how you play these theatres. I learnt the most from Giles Havergal, who gave me my first job at the Citizens Theatre, Glasgow, and from my time at the newest old theatre in this book, Shakespeare's Globe. On most evenings, Giles instinctively stood at the front of his theatre with the humblest employees, the ticket-takers, welcoming the audience as if they were part of his company. His director's office was located beside the stalls, front of house, and we often saw him backstage in the staff dining room or rehearsal room. Everything was contained within that one old building, and the crown touched the feet so to speak; the governor walked amongst us, all of us, knew us all by name. I relate this tangential history of Mr Havergal as he seems to me always to have been the finest director of a theatre I have ever encountered, because he made a true circle of the audience and artists, inspired I propose by the architecture of his old theatre.

Shakespeare's theatre inspired me alike, but on stage as well as off. Unable to turn off the sun in the daytime I saw my audience for the first time. Saw, for the most part, their innocence and willingness for the play. In the dark I had projected onto them my own criticism and disbelief. Thrust, on the Globe stage, into the middle of the circle of shared light, in an age before steel allowed the architects to throw forward the galleries and push the actors behind a proscenium, I realised the single most important lesson I have ever learnt as an actor. I must play with the audience, not at them, for them or to them . . . with them, with their imagination, as fellow players. I was amongst them, part of a circle, a storytelling circle. They were at the same table, in the same room, around the same imaginative fire of whatever story we had lit.

This lesson served me well in all other theatres since. It is why I object to lighting and sound equipment occupying the boxes of West End theatres rather than people. I have it in my contract that the boxes must be used for the audience, so that the audience and actor can be seen together, completing the circle. Don't get me wrong, there are many aspects of modern technology that thrill me in the theatre, but the old theatres remind me that unless used carefully, technology can divide the room and remove the actor to another place. Impressive and powerful as that may be, the greatest moments for me, as actor or audience, have been when actor and audience have become one. That is what I go to experience in all these wonderful theatres.

Do you notice the straight lines of rationality creeping into the modern auditoriums of this book, the removal of boxes and curved rows of seats? Nothing but technology if a young Hamlet looks up in search of a circular design in the heavens. The auditoriums are purposefully utilitarian in their décor as the lights will be turned off and the audience complained about if they make any inappropriate noise or movement. The old theatres celebrated the audience. The gaslights were never extinguished and no stage set could match the ornate and divinely inspired decoration of the auditorium. The audience were treated as gods. Creative gods. We actors live in their imagination.

I will treasure this book. The more you look at it and read, the more you learn. I hope that it will help to protect these architectural treasures of our nation of storytellers. We have lost so many. I hope we will lose no more and when we build anew, we will consider the designs by firelight!

Mark Rylance

Actor

# Introduction

*A Moment Towards the End of the Play* was the autobiography of the actor Timothy West, so-called after a monthly photographic feature in a theatre magazine, which always closed with a pictorial cliffhanger. This book suggests a moment or two before the start of a play – or musical – when you take stock of your surroundings and perhaps wonder about the history of the building, or its hidden features, its decoration, physical delights and atmosphere.

We have studied the exteriors, prowled the interiors, ascended to the upper circles and, above the stage, to the fly floors where the scenery is hoisted on hempen ropes or, increasingly, raised at the touch of a button; we have descended to the under-stage of carefully preserved Victorian wooden stage equipment and hydraulic lifts, and visited dressing rooms, cubby-holes and corners for lighting boards and electrical equipment . . . and then peered into royal boxes and retiring rooms, investigated corridors and orchestra pits, bars and foyers, before returning to the defining space of performance where the actors and the audience collide and mingle in the air-conditioned airiness (we hope) of the auditorium.

How the West End became 'Theatreland' – a definition first coined on a poster map of the Underground in 1915 – is to do with city planning and the need for new roads in the 1880s, and with a building programme that was driven by property speculation as much as by the public appetite for live entertainment. There were two earlier key phases, either side of the enforced closure of the theatres in 1642 by Oliver Cromwell's Long Parliament: the Elizabethan and Shakespearean age of playhouses in the city centre and south of the Thames; and the recovery during the Restoration of King Charles II in 1660 through to the Theatres Act of 1843, which green-lit the building first of the great music

*The Gielgud Theatre on Shaftesbury Avenue.*

*Inscription on the proscenium above the stage of the Richmond Theatre.*

halls, the theatres improper, and then of the theatres proper of the Victorians and Edwardians.

Theatre has ever since been a favourite national pastime, and our theatres – their buildings as much as their actors – the envy of the world. The historian John Earl, the first director of the campaigning organisation the Theatres Trust, has noted that at the beginning of the First World War every single large town or city in Britain had at least one, and more usually several, major theatres; 85 per cent of those thousand-or-so theatres were lost – through demolition, development or straightforward neglect – by 1980 in what is now called 'the great theatre massacre'.

There was devastation in London, too, over the years, and during the wars, but the West End has proved astonishingly resilient, re-inventing itself and spreading further afield into the countless fringe venues, of which the most prominent – the Donmar Warehouse in Covent Garden, the Young Vic in Waterloo and the Almeida in Islington, north London – form the creative engine room for much of what is best and most exciting in London theatre, alongside the Barbican, the National Theatre, the Open Air Theatre in Regent's Park and

Shakespeare's Globe, which now incorporates the exquisite indoor Sam Wanamaker Playhouse.

The history of our theatre, and its buildings, is one of bifurcation in the performing arts. The two strands of serious drama and musical, or indeed music hall, entertainment have their roots in the Restoration, when King Charles granted just two royal patents, or licences: one to the dramatist and theatre manager Thomas Killigrew and the King's Company at Drury Lane; the other to the poet laureate William D'Avenant and the Duke's Company in Lincoln's Inn Fields, relocating to the Theatre Royal in Covent Garden, newly built by the manager John Rich from his profits on John Gay's *The Beggar's Opera*, the first major British musical.

These two Theatres Royal, in Drury Lane and Covent Garden – where the flower and vegetable market had recently been established – therefore retained a virtual monopoly on serious drama. So lighter entertainment and variety, with singing and dancing, started sprouting in some other 'disreputable' theatres, as well as in pubs, upstairs rooms and various informal locations. In 1707, Her Majesty's in the Haymarket was finally licensed to present opera and musical plays and was therefore London's first opera house, while in 1766 the Haymarket Theatre itself was given a summer licence for the period each year when Drury Lane and Covent Garden shut up shop. The next summer patent was granted to the Lyceum Theatre in order to help out Drury Lane, which had burned down in 1809; theatres were destroyed by fire or demolished quite regularly throughout the eighteenth and nineteenth centuries and often – as in the case of Drury Lane – rebuilt on the same site.

Even though the Theatres Act, making licences more readily available from the Lord Chamberlain, might have led to more and more serious drama, the public's appetite for the hybrid nature of variety had been whetted and now the first purpose-built music halls were built in south London, in Lambeth and Southwark. Five big supper room music halls followed in the 1850s and 1860s, among them Evans in Covent Garden (part of the story of the Charing Cross Theatre) and the Alhambra in Leicester Square; their popularity only increased when dance was abandoned by the opera houses and ballet moved into the music hall.

Meanwhile, Theatreland was evolving along the Strand from Charing Cross to Fleet Street, with eleven playhouses materialising, including the Vaudeville and the Savoy, and others further to the west, including the Criterion, Prince of Wales and Playhouse. The building boom between 1880 and 1915 signals the true making of the West End. Shaftesbury Avenue and Charing Cross Road were created in 1886–7, with eight theatres arising on the Avenue in the next twenty-four years, and four more on Charing Cross Road. The Aldwych and Kingsway opened in 1905, with many theatres built, and now gone; eleven new West End theatres were constructed on new sites after 1924 and, between 1929 and 1937, the Adelphi, the Savoy and the Prince of Wales were recast in a modern style. In the 1950s and 1960s, six West End theatres, including the historic St James's, were swallowed up by the property developers.

In the boom Victorian/Edwardian period, there were several architects who defined our theatre for the twentieth century and beyond. The first great theatre specialist, and acknowledged doyen, was C.J. Phipps, responsible for Sadler's Wells, the Haymarket, Savoy and Her Majesty's. The most prominent, prolific and original – less classically trained than Phipps – was Frank Matcham, son of a brewery manager in Devon, who married the daughter of J.T. Robinson, architect of the Old Vic, and built countless beautiful theatres throughout the UK before hitting the West End and putting up the great variety houses – the Coliseum,

the Palladium, the Hackney Empire – for the biggest managements.

Matcham passed on something of his own improvisatory flair and engineering know-how – for instance, he introduced cantilevered galleries (with no supporting pillars) – to both Bertie Crewe (who trained in London and Paris and designed the Royal Court with the venerable Walter Emden) and W.G.R. Sprague, a master of matching Renaissance frontages to perfectly scaled interiors. Sprague, who was of Australian descent, and successively articled to both Matcham and Emden for a total of seven years, designed four 'pairs' of West End theatres: Wyndham's and the New (now the Noël Coward), Aldwych and the Strand (the Novello), the Globe (the Gielgud) and the Queen's, the Ambassadors and St Martin's.

In 1972, the Greater London Council planned to redevelop Covent Garden, threatening sixteen theatres and probably ripping the heart out of Theatreland. Fearing the worst, the Covent Garden Market decamped to Nine Elms in Vauxhall. But the theatre stood firm, or at least resolute. A Save London Theatres Campaign was instrumental in defeating the GLC's plans, rescued the Shaftesbury Theatre (where the plaster ceiling had collapsed overnight during the run of *Hair*) and led to the foundation of the Theatres Trust in 1976.

Many theatres were now given Grade II listings, thus protecting them from both demolition and other usage. For a time, though, the future of the fabric of London theatre seemed uncertain. A Theatres Trust report of 2003 estimated that £250 million needed to be spent in order to bring the West End theatres up to date. Government agencies such as the Arts Council, the Heritage Lottery Fund and the London Development Agency were, and are, committed to supporting theatres in the subsidised sector, such as the National Theatre and the Royal Court. The West End is a commercial operation, and always has been; theatres were built in the first place to make money for their owners.

But the last twenty years has seen a remarkable turnaround, both in the philosophy of theatrical architecture – West End theatres, thought by some to be unfit for purpose, have been appreciated again as answering the modern requirement of bringing more faces closer to the action because of their predominantly wrap-around, horseshoe design – and in the determination of theatre owners and producers to invest their profits in a still-thriving sector back into the buildings themselves. Figures from the Society of London Theatres reveal that 14 million people a year spend upwards of £500 million on theatre tickets. West End attendances rose by 26 per cent between 1986 and 2012, and revenues by 347 per cent. The financial benefit of this activity to the community, in terms of tourism, small satellite businesses and manufacturing firms, let alone in taxes paid to the government, is incalculable.

The other crucial factor in all this is that, while mixed and social media run riot through our culture and our leisure-time, the importance and the value of 'live' performance – that indissolubly powerful bind between artists and audience in the same room at one particular time – has increased, exponentially. And we have learned to love our old theatres all over again, especially as some of the new ones made us realise what we could soon be missing.

The turnaround began in earnest when the impresario Bernard Delfont asked Cameron Mackintosh if he would take over the two theatres he owned, the Prince Edward and the Prince of Wales. He wanted them taken into safekeeping for the future. Mackintosh agreed on condition that his new joint venture with Delfont would be committed to revitalising those theatres. Then the owners of the Strand Theatre made a similar overture and Mackintosh found himself on a lengthening path of restoration. By the end of 1991, Delfont's First Leisure theatre division was incorporated in a new company, Delfont Mackintosh Theatres Ltd. Delfont died in 1994.

DMT Ltd now owns eight West End theatres outright, and has spent millions on their restoration, refurbishment, improvement and modernisation, while always mindful of the architectural and design qualities inherent in the buildings. Many of the DMT theatres tell their own stories on the walls and along the corridors. And the rest of the West End has followed suit. Andrew Lloyd Webber's Really Useful Group owns seven theatres, including the flagship Drury Lane and Palladium houses, while Nimax – a company name derived from those of producer Nica Burns and American producer and investor Max Weitzenhoffer – owns six, with another one on the way. The fourth big player in the ownership stakes is the massive international Ambassador Theatre Group, which owns forty theatres across the world, eleven of them in the West End.

While ATG has done some admirable restoration work on many of its theatres, the worry is that the volatility in the company's operation and executive appointments might lead to instability of ownership and continuity. But theatre people remain at the top of the organisation, even if the real power, and the real money, is lurking in the shadows. At the opposite end of the spectrum, the Haymarket and the St Martin's have remained in private, individual ownership. In the subsidised, or public, sector, lines are now blurred between support from the taxpayer through the Arts Council and other channels, and through sponsors, donors and charitable funding bodies. The National Theatre, for instance, which has 30 per cent of its income from the state (in 1980, that figure was 60 per cent), raises £6 million a year in sponsorship and donations; in its recent £80 million rebuild and refit, one individual sponsor gave a cool £10 million, so they renamed one of their three auditoria after him.

While Mackintosh and his peers and colleagues have been busy restyling the West End as 'fit for purpose' (as far as is practically possible), some of the most spectacular redesigning and improvement work has been around such temples of contemporary performance as the Royal Court and Sadler's Wells, while smaller London theatres have benefited from new trends in what Steve Tompkins of Haworth Tompkins, one of the key architects in theatre renovation – he's been deeply involved in the Royal Court, the Young Vic, the Donmar and the National – calls 'a stripped back aesthetic'. Exposed brickwork and a rawness of finish is a feature common to both the Royal Court and Wilton's Music Hall. The miracle of what's happened at Wilton's is a comment not only on the campaigners who saved the building and then raised the money, but on the growing awareness of what places like Wilton's can offer, not least in keeping a handle on our cultural identity and understanding the roots of our theatre.

Over these past three decades, the London theatre structure has not ossified and decayed, but changed and evolved, far beyond what we might have expected. Not only that, there is more to come. The former director of the National Theatre, Nicholas Hytner, is opening a new warehouse-style theatre, The Bridge, seating 900 people, on the ground floor of a new apartment block adjacent to Tower Bridge. And Cameron Mackintosh is not only re-opening the Victoria Palace, a great Frank Matcham theatre, after a £30 million rebuild, but he also plans to refashion the Ambassadors, first home of *The Mousetrap*, the longest-running play in British theatre history, and rename it the Sondheim Theatre in honour of the American composer of *A Little Night Music* and *Sweeney Todd*.

Not to be outdone, Nimax are building a new 600-seat theatre on Charing Cross Road, due to open when the new Crossrail system of trains for London and the south-east of England is complete, some time soon after 2020; this as-yet unnamed theatre will be situated right by the former Astoria dance club, once a theatre (it opened in 1977 with a show about Elvis Presley), formerly a cinema and, until 1921, a factory producing pickles and jams for the Crosse

*Stage door, Palace Theatre.*

& Blackwell company. Just as the West End was originally formed to improve the transport system of cars and cabs by creating new roads, so the new system of Crossrail is to be saluted by a new theatre fortuitously constructed on one of those same West End defining roads.

Any theatre building is doubly potent as a house of dreams and a palimpsest of past occupation. This book is not a gazetteer, but a deliberate choice of Peter Dazeley and myself among a cornucopia of options, an *embarras de richesses* that have delighted and intrigued us, as we hope they will you, too. We are Londoners, and the story of London Theatres is not only a story of great buildings in an ever-changing city, but also a story of our cultural past and future in the city's geography and architecture, and in the lives of our fellow citizens, children, visitors and guests.

Performances are embalmed in the lineaments of the theatres that engender them. But they echo, too, down the years and across the generations, memorable performances in perfect settings: John Gielgud as Chekhov's Ivanov at the Phoenix, Laurence Olivier as Othello at the Old Vic, Paul Scofield as Sir Thomas More in *A Man for All Seasons* at the Globe (now the Gielgud), Vanessa Redgrave in Ibsen's *Lady from the Sea* at the Roundhouse, Judi Dench and Ian McKellen in *Macbeth* at the Donmar Warehouse, Mark Rylance in *Farinelli and the King* in the Sam Wanamaker, or as Olivia in *Twelfth Night* in Shakespeare's Globe, Billie Piper in *Yerma* at the Young Vic, Juliet Stevenson and Lia Williams in *Mary Stuart* at the Almeida. You think about these performances, and you think of them in their surroundings, in their theatres, physically pinned, but, in the mind's eye, still flickering.

GRANDES DAMES

# Royal Opera House

There have been three theatres on the north-east angle of Inigo Jones's Covent Garden piazza since 1732, each of them of increasing size and importance, and still the work of improvement and rebuilding goes on. The theatre now standing is, essentially, the third house, designed by Edward M. Barry (son of Charles Barry, architect of the Palace of Westminster) in 1858 after a fire broke out in the second theatre in the small hours of 5 March 1856 at the end of a drunken masked ball.

The Greek portico on Bow Street was already in place, but Barry designed a new fire-proof structure with a horseshoe plan auditorium, boxes enclosing the pit and the pit stalls with an amphitheatre above and side galleries. That is exactly what you see today. And Barry supplied, too, the adjacent Winter Garden annexe, the Floral Hall, an Italianate cast-iron structure damaged by fire in 1956 but carefully restored and now the showpiece of the 1999 restoration designed by Dixon Jones that took three years to complete and cost £214 million. The manager of the 1858 theatre was Frederick Gye, whose marble statue remains prominent in the foyer alongside two other important memorials: a bust of the conductor Thomas Beecham, who was associated with the house for over forty years; and a stone tablet for Vivien Duffield, chair of the 1999 development appeal. There's a blue dome in the foyer and red and gold lamps; red and gold, with cream, constituted Barry's colour scheme in the auditorium, and that is reproduced today, creating an atmosphere of unfussy plushness amid all the brass fittings and polished wood around the aisles and corridors.

Barry's grand staircase and crush bar are unaltered, though the crush bar (so-called not because of the crowds but because of the availability there of an orange and lemon crush drink in

PREVIOUS PAGE AND LEFT *Auditorium of the Royal Opera House, looking much the same as it did in 1858.*

*The royal box.*

the nineteenth century) is now the 'crush room' for private dining, the majority audience's pre-show and interval dining and drinking facilities having moved across to the sensationally enhanced and enlarged Floral Hall, now named for the sponsor Paul Hamlyn. From there you can take an escalator to the amphitheatre which has a fine curvilinear bar of its own, with more dining facilities and a rooftop loggia overlooking the piazza, with not-too-distant views of Nelson's Column, St Martin's-in-the-Fields and the London Eye. What a transformation this part of London has seen, one accelerated in recent decades by the removal of the market to Nine Elms, and largely dictated by the building of theatres over three centuries.

Covent Garden should rightly be called 'Convent' Garden, as it stands on the site of a medieval nunnery. The flower and vegetable market took root in the mid-seventeenth century, around the time when King Charles II granted, in 1660, at the start of the monarchy's Restoration, two theatre patents: one to Thomas Killigrew and the King's Company at Drury Lane, the other to the poet laureate William D'Avenant and the Duke's Company in Lincoln's Inn Fields. In 1732, after a spell in Dorset Gardens, it relocated with D'Avenant's patent to the Theatre Royal in Covent Garden, built by the manager John Rich from his profits on John Gay's *The Beggar's Opera*. The composer Handel, who had lived in England since 1712, was closely associated with the theatre as both composer and organist. Many of his operas were performed there. The English premiere of *The Messiah* in 1743 did not go as well as it had done in Dublin the year before, but the 1749 revival was better received and Handel had the satisfaction of hearing it again, now an acclaimed masterpiece, in the same theatre just ten days before he died in 1759. The theatre was subtly renamed the Theatre Royal, Covent Garden, in 1769 and had extensive alterations made – and premieres of Goldsmith's *She Stoops to Conquer* (1773) and Sheridan's *The Rivals* (1775) – before it was destroyed by fire in 1808, killing twenty-three firemen as the building collapsed.

The new theatre, with its portico designed by Robert Smirke, architect of the British Museum, opened just eight months later in 1809 with a performance of *Macbeth* starring the brother and sister team of John Philip Kemble and Sarah Siddons. To try and recoup costs, seat prices were raised, leading to public uproar and the reading of the Riot Act from the stage. After sixty-one disrupted performances, Kemble submitted to protest, made a formal apology, and lowered the prices. Siddons had come to Covent Garden after twenty years as Queen of Drury Lane. Lady Macbeth was her most famous role. She played it at her farewell performance in Covent Garden on 29 June 1812. At the end of the sleepwalking scene, the audience stopped the show with tumultuous applause. Eventually, the curtain parted and Siddons, now in her own clothes and character, made an emotional farewell speech lasting eight minutes.

Other milestones in the second theatre's existence were the revolution in stage lighting with the introduction of limelights in 1837; and, in 1841, the invention of the box set – i.e., a room on the stage with the fourth wall down so the audience can see in – for *London Assurance* by Dion Boucicault, produced by Madame Vestris. A playwright called Tom Robertson loved this innovation so much that he started to write plays specifically for box sets, thus instigating our drawing room comedy tradition of a hundred years.

In 1843, the Theatres Act ended the patent theatres' monopoly of drama, and competition for audiences intensified. So when a company of opera singers walked out of Her Majesty's in a huff in early 1847, the theatre underwent a quick remodelling of its auditorium and re-opened in April of the same year as the Royal Italian Opera, with a performance of Rossini's *Semiramide*.

When Barry's new theatre opened after the fire in 1858 with Meyerbeer's *Les Huguenots*, the future of British opera production was assured, almost. In 1892, as the repertoire broadened, the theatre was renamed the Royal Opera House, but the two world wars disrupted progress. During the first, the place was used as a furniture repository and, during the second, as a Mecca dance hall; it might have stayed that way but for the acquisition of the lease by the music publishers Boosey and Hawkes, who installed David Webster as the General Administrator. The ROH re-opened in 1946 with Sadler's Wells Ballet as resident ballet company and an embryo Covent Garden Opera, both companies eventually awarded royal charters: the Royal Ballet in 1956, the Royal Opera in 1968. The past had at last caught up with the present. The facilities were considered inadequate from the early 1980s, when the development scheme was put in motion but not fully activated until the creation of the National Lottery and an award of £58.5 million, about a third of the required amount, towards the rebuilding costs.

Work started in 1996. There are now new technical facilities and light-filled rehearsal rooms making the most of the island site across two complete urban blocks that was acquired when the market departed. All the early-twentieth-century hydraulically operated bridges, cycloramas and thunder runs are long gone but the scene dock and storage capacity, as well as the technical updates, are unmatched in London (although a lot of set building goes on in a warehouse in Thurrock, Essex). All the dance studios have sprung floors, there's an on-site gymnasium with physiotherapy, and a wardrobe where the costume support extends to maintaining clothes in dance and opera productions dating back forty or even fifty years. There are ten floors in the building (and sixty pianos), 1,000 people work there, with an opening night roughly every ten days. The rebuild also included two new studio theatres, the 420-seat Linbury and the informal 200-seat Clore.

The Linbury auditorium, steeply raked and awkwardly arranged, is important for experimental new work and visiting companies, the Clore for the company's extensive education programme. The former is one main target of the latest Open Up development: it will be remodelled into a far more flexible space. There are to be new toilet facilities, a new foyer for the Linbury, and something done about the main foyer which, despite its marvellous heavy wooden doors and portals to the stalls, and five pairs of plaster cherubs fitted with golden wings, remains a difficult area for patrons to negotiate, never quite sure which way to turn, or indeed look, when they first enter the premises through the remains of the early Victorian vestibule.

Royal Opera House
Bow Street, London WC2E 9DD
www.roh.org.uk

*The lighting brackets lowered to stage level.*

# Theatre Royal Haymarket

One of only three Grade I listed theatres in London – the others are the Theatre Royal, Drury Lane, and the Royal Opera House – the Theatre Royal, Haymarket, is a lovingly maintained family theatre of undiminished splendour and ideal playhouse proportions, now restored to the 1904 Louis XVI decorative scheme inside the John Nash 1821 theatre, the third built on the site, with a seating capacity of 890.

A royal patent was granted for the showing of serious plays in 1767, thus breaking the monopoly of Drury Lane and Covent Garden, and this was the last London theatre – in the 1960s – to play the National Anthem before the show and to serve teas on trays in the matinée intervals. In fact, the first ever matinée was given at the Haymarket; it was the first theatre endowed with what are known as foyers; and, in the 1880s, the Haymarket was the first theatre to pay high (verging on exorbitant) salaries to leading players.

The Haymarket of the 1880s and 1890s, with its classical portico, gilded proscenium, corridors, painted classical scenes and sparkling chandelier, was the fiefdom of one of the last great actor-managers, Herbert Beerbohm Tree. He was in charge from 1888 to 1896, then went on to build the theatre across the road, Her Majesty's, on the profits from George du Maurier's *Trilby*, in which he starred as the literally hypnotic Jewish piano player Svengali in 1895. The Haymarket became the natural home of Oscar Wilde, always a box office draw, whose *A Woman of No Importance* and *An Ideal Husband* were premiered under the ever-spreading Tree.

But the theatre's origins were far from grand and lie in the growth of the Haymarket from the muck and stables of the late sixteenth century to the fine houses laid out for the Earl of Suffolk at the end of the seventeenth. In 1720, on the site of an

*View from the royal box.*

*The ceiling of the auditorium.*

inn on the Haymarket (The King's Head) and a gun shop in Suffolk Street to the rear, a local carpenter, John Potter, built a playhouse known as the Little Theatre in the Hay. Satires by Henry Fielding attacking political parties and caricaturing the royal family led to the Licensing Act of 1737 (and Fielding's career as a novelist) and the closure of the theatre. This Act was not repealed until 1968 with the demise of censorship by the Lord Chamberlain's office. But the enterprising and colourful manager Samuel Foote by-passed the law by inviting 'friends' in for cups of chocolate and entertainment.

The almost-forgotten Foote, a foul-mouthed, one-legged Cornish comedian, was memorialised by the actor Ian Kelly in a 2015 play *Mr Foote's Other Leg* (adapted from his own book), which transferred, appropriately enough, from Hampstead Theatre to the Haymarket in Richard Eyre's production with Simon Russell Beale. Foote lost his leg after breaking it in a riding accident, and as it was audibly sawn

off by a surgeon, Russell Beale commented that it would be 'bloody hard to top that in the second act'. It was, but the point was that the Duke of York, whose horse Foote was riding at the time of the accident, secured a compensatory license for him to perform drama during the summer months when the two patented theatres were closed; hence the third Theatre Royal in 1767, next door to the Little. Foote died ten years later.

In 1805, hundreds of tailors protested at a revival of Foote's satire *The Tailors*, their rioting only quelled when the troops went in. Foote was always pillorying the fashions of the day, and used to appear on stage himself as an overly made-up, heavily upholstered wannabe fashionista, so it's a lovely irony that the latest phase of the Haymarket's existence stems from the ownership of the lease by a fashion industry mogul, Louis Michaels. After Foote, Nash's 1821 classical rebuild – portico, arched doorways, pit, boxes and galleries – was part of a regeneration scheme in the area. Extensive alterations in 1843 led to the stage being pushed back to allow for more expensive orchestra stalls and the abolition of the pit. Under the management of J.B. Buckstone between 1853 and 1877, the Haymarket became the leading high comedy theatre of the day (2 p.m. matinées were a Buckstone innovation) and he was succeeded by two more legendary figures in the Haymarket's history, Squire Bancroft in 1879 – who commissioned C.J. Phipps to remodel the interior, reseat the audience and create the first ever picture-frame proscenium that still glistens in the blue and gold auditorium – and then Tree. At the turn of the century, there was more modernisation, while the nineteenth-century stage machinery remained stowed in a deep cellar behind the proscenium. A new sliding stage was installed between the two world wars.

The big lounge bar under the stalls, now with a small bar at either end, was created in 1939. The modern actor most associated with the Haymarket, John Gielgud, actually resided in the star dressing room (the Number Ten) during the war and appointed himself fire-warden to the theatre; he appeared in five plays in his great repertory season of 1944/5 – *Hamlet*, *A Midsummer Night's Dream*, *Love for Love*, *The Duchess of Malfi* and Somerset Maugham's *The Circle* – and this heralded a procession of famous productions including Ralph Richardson and Peggy Ashcroft in *The Heiress* (1949), Noël Coward and Margaret Leighton in Shaw's *The Apple Cart* (1954), Edith Evans and Ashcroft in Enid Bagnold's *The Chalk Garden* (1956), Maggie Smith and Joan Plowright in *The Way of the World* (1984) and Jack Lemmon and Kevin Spacey in Eugene O'Neill's *Long Day's Journey Into Night* (1986).

*The Haymarket is fully restored to its 1904 Louis XVI decorative scheme.*

The freehold is owned by the Crown Estate. Louis Michaels, who sold his Cavendish fashion business to the House of Fraser, acquired the lease in 1971, together with his partner, Enid Chanelle. Chanelle's daughter married the current lessee, Arnold Crook, whose own business background was in textiles. Michaels, who had launched the West End producing company Triumph with Paul Elliott and Duncan Weldon, created a star-laden programme that operated in a nexus of the Haymarket and Chichester Festival Theatre under Laurence Olivier's successors, John Clements, Keith Michell and Peter Dews. By the time Crook succeeded Michaels (who died in 1981) as chairman, the idea of a Haymarket play, prevalent for decades, was beginning to fray, and the audience no different, really, from any other theatre's. Crook's response was to inaugurate, in 2007, adventurous classical seasons by short-term artistic directors – Jonathan Kent, Sean Mathias and Trevor Nunn – a model for other managements presenting seasons supervised by Michael Grandage at Wyndham's, Jamie Lloyd at the Trafalgar Studios (formerly the Whitehall Theatre) and Kenneth Branagh at the Garrick Theatre.

The Haymarket retains its glorious pre-eminence in this ever-changing, ever-evolving West End. The theatre closed for six months in 1994 for a major refurbishment, part of Crook's deal to retain the lease from the Crown Commission. Gold leaf worth £1 million was applied where needed, the 1821 stage roof trusses overhauled and reinforced, the two tapestries in the stalls cleaned up, as were 2,000 lead crystals in the main chandelier, and the paintings on the ceiling given the full cotton bud treatment. A few years ago, the stalls seats and carpeting were replaced, and the two circles and gallery – where one used to sit on perilously hard and uncomfortable wooden benches – all re-upholstered. There are sixty on-site employees, every office crammed with activity, right into the building's dramatic attic.

The Queen Mother, who died in 2002, was a regular visitor. Attending on her birthday in 1992 to see Rex Harrison in Shaw's *Heartbreak House*, she requested only that the National Anthem should be played. Late in the day, the administration realised that they didn't have it on tape, so Arnold Crook ordered his general manager, Nigel Everett, to stand at the back of the royal circle and strike up a solo rendition of 'Happy Birthday'. Luckily, the audience joined in, and all was well: 'We thought your birthday should take precedence over patriotism, Ma'am,' beamed a relieved Crook. When she returned a few years later to see Patricia Routledge as Lady Bracknell, Crook asked if he could help her to the box by lifting her skirt. 'That's the best offer I've had all day,' she replied.

Theatre Royal Haymarket
18 Suffolk Street, London SW1Y 4HT
www.tfh.co.uk

OPPOSITE

ABOVE *The royal receiving room, built for Queen Victoria upon her request.*
BELOW *The royal box, close to the stage, as seen from the stalls.*

# Theatre Royal Drury Lane

The grand old lady of Drury Lane, who actually opens her doors onto little Catherine Street, is the historic home of Nell Gwyn, Restoration drama and the significant Shakespeare revival, David Garrick, Sarah Siddons, Edmund Kean, Lord Byron, Sheridan the playwright, the legendary clown Joey Grimaldi, spectacular Victorian pantomime, the inter-war melodic musical extravaganzas of Ivor Novello and the great post-war American musicals of Rodgers and Hammerstein: *Oklahoma!* (1947), *Carousel* (1950), *South Pacific* (1951) and *The King and I* (1953).

This is the greatest story ever told in the West End, and it's related in the architecture of a building that is the fourth built on approximately the same site, with much the same vast auditorium it was given in 1922. It boasts the enhanced Regency splendour of a spectacular rotunda, rival royal boxes and a grand saloon (now with an outdoor terrace over the 1820 neoclassical portico) decorated with paired Corinthian columns and pilasters, an apse at either end of the room, and statues of favourite sons in the dark wooden and marble foyer – those of a formally posed Shakespeare and reclining Noël Coward. Coward, whose wartime chronicle *Cavalcade* opened here in 1931, sports a cravat, crossed legs and idly wafted cigarette in Angela Conner's brass likeness, donated by Coward's lover Graham Payn and unveiled by the Queen Mother in 1998.

At the Restoration of the monarchy, King Charles II granted a royal patent to just two theatres – Thomas Killigrew's Drury Lane and Covent Garden – which separated them from the rest doing low comedy, vaudeville and circuses. The Lane was closed by the Plague in 1663, a fifteen-year-old Nell Gwyn made her debut in 1665, the theatre was consumed by fire in 1672 but re-opened, designed by Christopher Wren, in 1674. In 1735,

*The auditorium from the King's royal box, looking across to the Prince Regent's box, which is identified by a fleur-de-lys.*

Charles Macklin had a backstage row with a fellow actor, Thomas Hallam, over the vexed issue of wigs, and poked his eye out with a stick; he claimed the murder was an accident and that he had only urinated on Hallam's body as an attempt at antisepsis.

Garrick arrived in 1742 for his thirty years of unadulterated fame, speaking Samuel Johnson's renowned prologue in 1747:

> Ah! Let not Censure term our Fate our Choice
> The Stage but echoes back the publick Voice
> The Drama's Laws the Drama's Patrons give
> For we that live to please, must please to live.

He sold his shares on to Sheridan in 1776. Sheridan's comic masterpiece *The School for Scandal* followed in the following year. Garrick not only revolutionised acting, he redesigned (or Robert Adam did) the interior, did away with audience members on the stage, and dimmed the lights on the house. Garrick, more than anyone else, in these matters

and in his acting, is the father of our modern theatre.

The theatre was declared unsafe in 1790, demolished, rebuilt, and burned to the ground again in 1809, with co-owner Sheridan stoically raising a glass to the leaping flames and occasional explosion in the comfort of a Westminster coffee house, defending his sanguinary stance to his fellows thus: 'A man may surely be allowed to take a glass of wine beside his own fireside.' The new theatre opened with a prologue by Lord Byron in 1812, gas lighting was introduced in 1817 and yet another rebuild in 1832 prompted Dickens, who became a devotee of Grimaldi and Victorian pantomime, to herald 'the oldest as it is also the largest and handsomest of the theatres proper in London'. Indeed it was. The era of wild man Edmund Kean ('Seeing him act', said Coleridge, was 'like reading Shakespeare by flashes of lightning') and master clown Grimaldi was marked by an imposing colonnade of Corinthian pillars along the Russell Street side in 1831, and the introduction of limelights to focus on solo performers. With the advent of the King of Pantomime, Augustus 'Druriolanus' Harris,

*The star's dressing room.*

*Gordon Aldred's backdrop paintframe studio, backstage.*

in 1879, a lull in the theatre's fortunes was transformed by spectacular scenic productions, the drafting in of Marie Lloyd (waving to the boy who's 'up in the gallery' before she 'sits among the cabbages and peas'), Vesta Tilley and other music hall stars and, in 1894, the installation of hydraulically operated under-stage machinery that remains in place, and in action, to this day.

You can absorb the physical phenomena and extant machinery of the place in a public tour conducted by well-informed actors. Under the front three rows of the stalls there's one of four subterranean brick tunnels dating from the first theatre in 1663, one of which, it's said, took the King directly into the Strand to meet Nell Gwyn on the site of the tavern in Bull Inn Court (next door to the Adelphi) that bears her name still. (Unfortunately, this seems unlikely, as the tunnel would have been at least half a mile long and water levels have altered too much around that area for such a facility to be topographically plausible.) The great history of twentieth-century musical theatre is celebrated in a poster display in the stalls bar – from *Show Boat* with Paul Robeson in 1928, through Novello's 'glamorous nights', *My Fair Lady* (1958) with Rex Harrison and Julie Andrews, *A Chorus Line* (1976), Stephen Sondheim's *Sweeney Todd* (1980) and *Miss Saigon* (1989) which ran for ten years. In corridors running either side of the grand circle you can see the unexploded bomb that fell right through the theatre in October 1940, a copy of the royal patent and a glimpse of the gilt, gold and red plush royal box anteroom where Frank Benson was knighted in 1916 by King George V during a tercentenary Shakespeare gala.

That anteroom is at the grand circle level of the great staircase in the Rotunda, restored to its Georgian green

*The 1947 painted backdrops to* Oklahoma!*, stored backstage.*

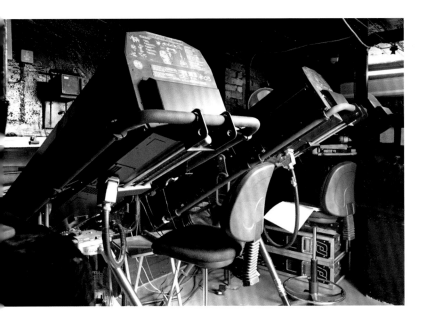

*Follow spotlights.*

*The anteroom of the royal box.*

paint and architectural elegance by Andrew Lloyd Webber's Really Useful Theatre Group when they acquired the theatre and spent £4 million on a refurbishment in 2013. One staircase is on the 'King's Side', the other on the 'Prince's Side', a legend which dates from a stand-up row in the foyer between mad King George III and his reprobate son, who both turned up one night for the same show and allowed their at-loggerheads default positions to boil over.

There are ghosts, too, of Grimaldi – one actor in a musical, the late Michael N. Harbour, claimed he was 'kicked in the arse' by the clown when he 'dried' – and of a 'man in grey' who emanates from the skeleton of a chap found in a circle alcove with a dagger through his heart, and even of a little girl with brown hair in the sub-stage.

You enter the rotunda, newly focused by Lloyd Webber's acquisition of Canova's *Three Graces* in white marble, from the vestibule. At ground level, are reproduction statues of Michael Balfe (composer of *The Bohemian Girl*), Garrick, Kean and Shakespeare again; on the upper level, more busts of the brewer Samuel Whitbread, who paid for Garrick's rebuild, the American Othello Ira Aldridge, actor Forbes Robertson and Novello. You descend to the circular stalls bar and the glories of the Empire-style auditorium decorated in pale blue-grey with Wedgwood blue and gold highlighting, three tiers of boxes either side of the strictly rectangular proscenium with an imitation lapis lazuli frame, often obscured in contemporary stage design. The sight of this arena is breathtaking whether unpopulated or full.

The scale is a perfect combination of vastness and intimacy. It is no accident that another great clown, Dan Leno, very different from Grimaldi, was one of the Lane's most popular successful performers, playing dame in pantomime for fifteen successive years from 1888. At just five feet tall he had, according to Marie Lloyd, 'the saddest eyes in the world', and could switch from comedy to pathos at the drop of a hat. And yet he filled the house, both literally and metaphorically. The critic William Macqueen-Pope said of him in 1960, 'There was only one Dan Leno, he never had a rival, and will never have a successor. He stands in the mighty frieze of Drury Lane alongside and equal with all of its great ones. . . . There is no statue to him there and no plaque, but almost everyone who enters remembers that this is where Dan Leno played.'

Theatre Royal Drury Lane

Catherine Street, London WC2B 5JF

www.reallyusefultheatres.co.uk

# Her Majesty's Theatre

Of all the tradesmen in our country who ever lived over their shop, surely none had as magnificent a post as Sir Herbert Beerbohm Tree, who occupied the dome of the Her Majesty's he had built for him by C.J. Phipps in 1897. He inhabited what became, on his watch, the most famous playhouse in Europe, until he died in 1917: in that period, Tree, the last of the great London actor-managers, produced, and usually acted in, sixteen elaborate and spectacular productions of Shakespeare and played opposite Mrs Pat Campbell in Shaw's *Pygmalion* in 1914. 'Not bloody likely' was heard in stunned silence before prompting laughter and applause that lasted over a minute. It echoes down the years as the first modern linguistic taboo-breaker.

It is appropriate that Tree's theatre should have become the home of *The Phantom of the Opera* for over thirty years. Like Tree, the Phantom hovered above the Paris Opéra, manipulating the voice of music in his unattainable soprano Christine Daaé, in much the same way as Svengali, Tree's most famous role, hypnotised his singing lover Trilby in the George du Maurier melodrama that made his fortune. And both *Phantom* and *Trilby* are variations on the same classical myth at the root of *Pygmalion*. Tree had been managing theatres in London for a decade before he used the profits made on *Trilby* across the road at the Haymarket to build his personal Xanadu, where the royal crest on a noble frontage suggested imperial allegiance in Queen Victoria's diamond jubilee year on the throne and audiences were attended by footmen in powdered wigs and liveries.

This was the fourth theatre on a site which had been the largest stable – and twice-weekly cattle market – on the Haymarket until, in 1705, John Vanbrugh decided on a theatre to rival Drury Lane in honour of Queen Anne, installing Thomas Betterton's company and the playwright William Congreve as manager. The Queen's Theatre (which became the King's in 1714 with the

*The auditorium capacity is 1,200, with an interior inspired by the opera house at Versailles, an appropriate environment for* The Phantom of the Opera.

accession of George I) was destroyed by a fire started by a disgruntled former employee in 1789. Two years later, it was rebuilt as the second largest opera house in Europe (after La Scala, Milan) and gave the London premieres of *Così fan tutte* and *The Magic Flute*. John Nash remodelled the building and added the still unspoilt Royal Opera Arcade to the rear in 1821, London's first shopping arcade with bow windows, big lanterns and circular sky lights, still an enclave of 'fine wine' stores and art galleries. Fourteen operas of Rossini received their British premieres in what was now the most expensive theatre in Britain, with seats costing a guinea, sometimes two, certainly when Jenny Lind sang Bellini's *Norma* in the late 1840s for Queen Victoria, whose beefeater guards stood on the stage. Now renamed Her Majesty's, the theatre was closed for four years in 1852 as Italian opera drifted away to Covent Garden, and was then consumed by fire once more in 1867. A third theatre (1868–91) was built within the remaining shell, and notably presented the first performance in England of Wagner's Ring Cycle in 1882. It was demolished in 1891, stripped at auction of its effects, leaving only the Nash arcade standing.

Phipps's theatre for Tree was (and still is) an imposing and glorious edifice in the French Renaissance style, and he paired it on the same block with the symmetrical addition of the luxury Carlton Hotel, similarly fronted and domed, which was badly damaged by wartime bombing, demolished in 1958 and replaced by the unapologetically Modernist New Zealand House in 1963. There is a fine canopy to the stone front and along the Charles II Street side, four Corinthian pillars above a balustrade fronting nine windows and a charming small foyer with a coffered ceiling, wood panelling and the commemoration stone laid by Tree's wife and help-mate, Maud Holt, on 16 July 1896.

The auditorium – and it's a much smaller, more intimate house than the previous two were, seating just 1,200 people – still has the same steel pillars supporting the two balconies, but the original cerise-coloured hangings and velvet pink seating have been superseded by a classical cream-painted and gold-finished interior and red seating arranged in a pleasing fan shape throughout on three levels. Three tiers of boxes are set between Corinthian pillars, and there are plaster busts of the poets among the fake marble pilasters. The very attractive dress circle bar opens onto the loggia above the Haymarket, and has portraits of the beautiful actresses Mabel Love and Dorothea Baird in, respectively, *The Three Musketeers* and *Trilby*. Under the stage is preserved the most important wooden Victorian theatre machinery in Britain – a series of lifts, levers, drums and winches give you a sense of being below decks at sea, and of how Tree magically grew complete forests on the stage, or the Senate of Rome, or a densely populated Runnymede for the signing of the Magna Carta scene interpolated into *King John*. High above at the fly floor level is the original wooden thunder run, a device fuelled by cannon balls dropped from the full height of a ladder but outstripped in modern usage first by thunder sheets and now by sound effects.

Tree's square copper dome (renewed in the 1990s) is approached through a pair of heavy wooden doors and reveals a high-ceilinged banquet room leading through to what were in effect his living quarters, where he also entertained his mistresses. His affair with a Mrs Reed of south London produced an illegitimate son: Carol Reed, the film director responsible for *Odd Man Out*, *The Third Man* and *Oliver!* and the uncle of the actor Oliver Reed. On the boat journey to his last long tour of the United States with his company in 1916, he surprised his daughter, the actress Viola Tree, by informing

her that she was about to meet his New York family. By then he had let the theatre to the producer Oscar Asche, who had been in his company since 1902; in 1916, Asche staged the Oriental Arabian Nights extravaganza-cum-pantomime *Chu Chin Chow*, the longest-running show in the British theatre until *The Mousetrap*, playing for five years and 2,235 consecutive performances.

The banquet room in the dome doubled as an office and rehearsal space, too, and it was here that Tree, tutoring his young actors in verse-speaking, founded RADA, the Royal Academy of Dramatic Art, in 1904, setting up the school in 1905 in the premises in Gower Street they still occupy today; Shaw gave the rights in *Pygmalion* in perpetuity to the new school. Meanwhile, Her Majesty's was evolving from a home of Italian opera, through Shakespeare and Shaw, to become the natural home of the intelligent modern musical that didn't need a barn full of 2,000 people to succeed. As a musical theatre playhouse, it proved perfect for the brilliant Shakespearean rewrite *West Side Story* in 1958 and the Jewish poverty and persecution show *Fiddler on the Roof* in 1967, both enjoying runs of several years, as well as for Stephen Sondheim's acidic metropolitan cartoon *Company*, which ran for a year in 1972. The director of *Company* was Harold Prince, who returned to the theatre as director of *Phantom*, providing, with designer Maria Bjornson, a replica of the Paris Opéra's gilt-and-caryatid proscenium on top of the Her Majesty's plaster frame, and replacing the theatre's chandelier – it's stowed, gathering dust, on the fly floor by the thunder run – with the special collapsible triple-decker chandelier for the show. This offers an effect worthy of Beerbohm Tree in his pomp. Tree's sub-stage timbers have been interlaced with modern machinery for the show; those parts of the mechanical forest not needed were removed, recorded, and will be reinstated when the *Phantom* flies on.

Her Majesty's Theatre

Haymarket, London SW1Y 4QL

www.reallyusefultheatres.co.uk

*The 'thunder run' in the stage left gallery is one of only two remaining in Britain; all the original stage machinery is of wooden construction.*

# Palace Theatre

The Palace is not the most beautiful theatre in London, but it is the most gothic, palatial, perpendicular, Victorian and vertiginous, an ideal home for Hogwarts, the school in *Harry Potter and the Cursed Child*, the first (five-hour, two-part) Harry Potter stage play, that has overtaken the interior and is likely to stay for a good many years yet. There is lots of marble, most of it concentrated on the great staircase in the vestibule that goes down to the stalls and up to the dress circle. And there's a sort of dustiness, too, about the place that is like a heartfelt exhalation of a rich, important history.

For this theatre, sitting proudly like a terracotta castle on a curve in Cambridge Circus, was intended to be, in 1891, the new home of English opera, a decisive move away from the Italian *bel canto* going off at Her Majesty's and Covent Garden. The impresario Richard D'Oyly Carte, who had made such a money-spinning success of Gilbert and Sullivan at the Savoy that he could build a hotel right next door to their shows, named his new folly the Royal English Opera House and announced a new grand opera by Arthur Sullivan, *Ivanhoe* (based on Walter Scott's novel), complete with horses, jousting, forest glades and waterfalls. Who knows what might have happened if *Ivanhoe*, presented in a single run of 160 performances, and containing some of Sullivan's loveliest music, hadn't simultaneously signalled the start and the end of the enterprise? But D'Oyly Carte had nothing to follow it with, and his dream crumbled. He rushed in a season of French opera and Sarah Bernhardt, then sold up to a company of which Augustus Harris, old 'Druriolanus' himself, was the managing director. Harris renamed it the Palace Theatre of Varieties in 1892, and the subsequent managements were those of Charles Morton and

Alfred Butt; all three of them are modestly commemorated in framed portraits outside the royal retiring room behind one of the dress circle boxes.

There were plenty of grandiose settings for variety already in the West End neighbourhood, notably the Hippodrome down the road at Leicester Square and the Coliseum in St Martin's Lane. Marie Tempest made her variety debut in 1906; the huge amphitheatre was reconstructed in 1908, leaving the auditorium looking much as it does today (seating for 1,400 people, over 300 of them in the huge, dramatically raked balcony, or upper circle) save for the removal of the stage boxes; the great prima ballerina Anna Pavlova made her first London appearance in 1910; and the renamed (in 1911) Palace Theatre hosted the first Royal Variety Performance in 1912. Revues and musical comedies, even a short period as a cinema, followed during and beyond the First World War, when *No, No, Nanette* (1925) – with hit songs 'Tea for Two' and 'I Want to be Happy' – ran for nearly two years.

So the story of the Palace is one of trying to make ends meet in a theatre designed for something else. Over its great history, as the possibility of grand British opera disappeared, big musicals fitted the bill best, notably Ivor Novello's *King's Rhapsody* (1949, 839 performances), *The Sound of Music* (1961, 2,385 performances), *Cabaret* (1968, 336 performances, with Judi Dench as Sally Bowles), *Jesus Christ Superstar* (1972, 3,358 performances) and *Les Misérables* (1985, running for nineteen years before moving on to the Queen's).

Andrew Lloyd Webber's Really Useful Theatre Group acquired the Palace in 1983 for £1.3 million. It had been on the open market because, as Emile Littler, who had managed the theatre for thirty-seven years, said in a short, emotional

*The main staircase in the imposing foyer on Cambridge Circus.*

hand-over speech that sounded like an echo of D'Oyly Carte, 'It is no good owning a theatre without things to put on the stage.' Lloyd Webber, now the only creative artist to own a theatre, certainly had 'things' to put on at the Palace, but, as a connoisseur and collector of Victorian art, notably the Pre-Raphaelite painters, he was even more messianic about restoring the architectural splendour of the place, inside and out, mindful of the poet John Betjeman's outrage that the veined marble pillars in the foyer had been 'defaced' in the 1950s with a coat of plum-coloured paint; when that paint was duly stripped off, the marble and Mexican onyx panels were revealed, undamaged. The vestibule was returned to its original glory, the brassy-coloured plaster mouldings on the ceiling restored, but not the William Morris carpets. At grand circle level, the marble starts to be a veneer, and there's no marble at all at the top in the balcony.

The Palace took two years to build – the foundation stone, laid by Helen D'Oyly Carte on 5 December 1888, is still visible to the right of the main entrance – with D'Oyly Carte supervising the master builder, G.H. Holloway, joined later by T.E. Collcutt, a renowned gothicist, to provide the architectural elaboration. The frontage, a triumph of balance and composition, meticulously cleaned and revealed afresh in 1987, was an intricate, fenestrated screen of Ellistown red brick and Doulton terracotta tiles – described by the eminent early-twentieth-century architect Sir Albert Richardson as 'the climax of the Reign of Terracotta' – with an internal ornamentation of figures and arches in the early Spanish Renaissance style. There were over 2,000 electric lamps powered by a generator on the premises, a proscenium arch of Italian marble with a tympanum above, now difficult to see, of allegorical figures.

Lloyd Webber took over the apartment at the top of the theatre formerly occupied by Emile Littler, and wrote much of his score for *The Phantom of the Opera* there, hoping to present the show in his own theatre. But *Les Misérables* had already dropped

*The auditorium commissioned by Richard D'Oyly Carte as the home of English opera.*

ABOVE *Harry Potter on the Palace Theatre façade.* OPPOSITE ABOVE *Rear stalls entrance.* OPPOSITE BELOW *Release for fire curtain, water drencher and stage lantern.*

anchor, and he was obliged to move across town to the Her Majesty's, which he also bought. In 2012 Lloyd Webber sold on the Palace to Nimax (Nica Burns and Max Weitzenhoffer) who have since reinforced the safety of the ceiling with a fine mesh membrane in a steel frame, onto which they project a copy of the painted ceiling above. Many performers attest to the surprising intimacy of so large a house. You get the best sense of this by either standing at the side of the balcony – the theatre is a sort of horseshoe, inside – or standing on the stage itself. It's high, but it's also narrow, and not too deep.

The lovely little balcony bar has been fitted out with countless clocks, all of them set at one minute to twelve, by the *Harry Potter* design team. This show has dictated the decoration of the auditorium, too, with the mirrors along the sides in the stalls wallpapered over in a blue-ish grey, with an 'HP' logo pattern which becomes a single 'H' for Hogwarts in the balcony on reddish paper.

Pride of place away from the vestibule is reserved for the stalls bar, an elegant, long, curved room, with a matching bar fronted in gold-painted plasterwork of cherubs and flora, and a small forest of white pillars at either end. Leading off

the bar is a small maze of corridors, polished wood, heavy doors and hidden stairways, lending further credence to the legend of four friendly ghosts on the premises, those of Pavlova, Ivor Novello (who appeared in *King's Rhapsody* here on the night he died), the manager Morton and another unnamed ballerina allegedly searching for a lost pair of pumps. There's even a spooky, abandoned wooden telephone kiosk and, even more oddly, two unexplained white ceramic dogs squatting in an alcove at first circle level. Under the stage, too, there's a haunted feel about the well-maintained but no longer practical wooden machinery, with clearly defined sloats, sliders and traps for scenery. At the very bottom, a pump used to keep the water level below the theatre (though the buried River Fleet does send up a constant supply of puddles) and the covered remains of an artesian well are dramatic reminders that much of London and many of its theatres are, in fact, floating on water.

Palace Theatre

Shaftesbury Avenue, London W1D 5AY

www.palacetheatrelondon.org

PLEASURE PALACES

# Shaftesbury Theatre

There is a nice conundrum attached to the Shaftesbury Theatre: it was both the first and the last theatre built on Shaftesbury Avenue, the thoroughfare created in 1887 to link Piccadilly Circus and New Oxford Street and continue the ongoing westward movement away from Drury Lane and Covent Garden. The first Shaftesbury Theatre, designed by C.J. Phipps, went up in 1888 on a plot of municipal land opposite Greek Street – there's a fire station there today – followed at the end of the year by the Lyric, then D'Oyly Carte's great Palace over the road, the Apollo, the Globe and the Queen's. It was destroyed in the Blitz in 1941.

The second Shaftesbury Theatre – on the remains of a maze of derelict property at the very top of the Avenue where it crosses the junction of St Giles and High Holborn – was so named in 1963, having started life in 1911 as the New Princes Theatre designed by Bertie Crewe, changing to the Princes Theatre in 1914. The shifting name implies no more similarity in the two theatres than in those that have shared the name of St James.

Phipps's theatre had been a handsome, square building of red brick and stone in the Italian style, a loggia on the first floor fronted by massive stone columns, with marble staircases and mosaic flooring inside, a balcony with a lounge at the back and seating for 1,800 people. The opening production was *As You Like It* starring the owner's wife and, in 1898, Londoners sampled American musical comedy for the first time with the *The Belle of New York*, which ran for two years. The theatre was established as the home of musicals, farce and light opera. After the bomb, the site was left derelict until a temporary fire station was set up to replace one that had been on the Avenue since 1921 and the new station was built in 1982.

PREVIOUS PAGE *The auditorium of the Shaftesbury Theatre, from the stage.*

LEFT *View from the dress circle.*

Crewe's less elegant creation, devised to house fashionable melodrama, is an imposing occupation of a corner site, faced in terracotta and brick stone with a three-storey façade of strictly aligned doors and windows, topped by a pillared cupola above the curve of the entrance that looks like an afterthought. The construction, though, was exceptional: this is the first entirely steel-framed theatre, with no pillars in an auditorium of real glamour and richness (at the front of the arena, at least), two cantilevered balconies and not a bad seat in the house – the whole of the huge dress circle, in an overall capacity of 1,400 seats, is sold at top price. The original colour scheme was cream and gold, and that has since been altered to pale peach and cream and then, in the 1980s, to rose pink, giving to the elaborate plasterwork the texture of a whipped dessert, like some surreal French ice cream.

The triumph of the interior is signalled in the two tiers of paired bow-fronted boxes, framed in Ionic pillars, with an arched tympanum showing scaled-up groups of figures representing Tragedy, Comedy, Poetry and Music. The headiness and frothiness of this visual treat never palls and is compounded with painted roundels of country scenes. The effect is slightly spoiled by the utilitarian black lantern boxes slung across the front of the upper circle by EMI when they bought the theatre in 1962 together with the property magnate and philanthropist Charles Clore, but these could (and should) be easily removed. The domed ceiling once had a huge mural sourced entirely from classical paintings in the National Gallery but that is now covered in white plaster, but you can still see through to the roof – which still opens. When the theatre opened in 1911, with *The Three Musketeers*, this was the escape route for the fumes and cigar smoke, and much needed it must have been, for Crewe was so caught up in filling the site with his theatre that he forgot about lounges and corridors and bars.

These facilities are cramped, as indeed is the foyer. The too-narrow bars are tacked

*The grid of steel cables and pulleys, the technical heart of the theatre high above the stage.*

on like extra limbs on the left-hand side, as if an indoor afterthought to match that of the outdoor cupola. But the successive managements of Seymour Hicks and Charles B. Cochran enjoyed great success here in the first quarter of the last century, with both light opera and ballet, and the Gershwins' *Funny Face*, whose run was interrupted in 1928 by an explosion in the gas-main pipes causing chaos across the West End. There was an even more localised mishap in 1973 when the ceiling collapsed overnight during the run of the rock musical *Hair*, an accident that prefigured a much more serious and similar dust-cloud accident – because it happened during a performance – at the Apollo Theatre in December 2013. Since then, more safety checks have been reinforced in all theatres.

The 1974 closure of the Shaftesbury very nearly led to its demolition. The timing was bad because in 1972 the Greater London Council had presented the development plan that frightened the Covent Garden fruit and vegetable market away from the centre (they decamped to Nine Elms) and threatened sixteen theatres, putatively tearing the heart out of the West End. It was in this context of architectural and political cynicism that the Shaftesbury was doubly imperilled, but the GLC plan was defeated, and the Shaftesbury saved – and given its Grade II listing – after some intense campaigning by the actors' union Equity and the newly formed Save London Theatres Campaign. The theatre came into the ownership of the impresario Laurie Marsh and the great farce producer Ray Cooney; when Cooney formed the Theatre of Comedy in 1983 – a loose alliance of actors and directors including Judi Dench, Maureen Lipman, Tom Conti and Donald Sinden – the company bought the theatre outright. By 1986 they were joined by the American producer Don Taffner, and the theatre has remained within the wing of his independent company, DLT Entertainment UK, ever since, Taffner Snr being succeeded by his son, Don Taffner Jnr, in 2011.

The Shaftesbury, which sits in the Bloomsbury Conservation area, has been improved by some striking structural innovations at a cost of £8 million, £5 million of which was raised through the controversial restoration levy fee most theatres now add on to the ticket price. Four steel columns, each taking 200 tons, now support a new fly tower, grid and set of offices; this rust-brown steel ziggurat of an extrusion – a striking saw-tooth box that was a result of the local authority demanding an architectural statement – appears to hover over the theatre roof, blending well enough with the surrounding skyscape of Victorian red brick and modern architecture, and has increased the theatre's appeal to Broadway musical producers with scenic and technical demands who wish to cross the pond after such crowd-pleasing visitors here as *Thoroughly Modern Millie*, *Hairspray*, *Memphis* and *Motown*.

Shaftesbury Theatre
210 Shaftesbury Avenue, London WC2H 8DP
www.shaftesburytheatre.com

# London Palladium

Many actors have 'died' on stage – failed to find favour with the audience – and some have literally dropped dead while performing, notably two great British entertainers: Tommy Cooper (at Her Majesty's) and Eric Morecambe (at the Roses Theatre in Tewkesbury), both in 1984; so it's perhaps fitting that the ashes of Morecambe's agent, Billy Marsh (1917– 95), are kept under the stage of the London Palladium, the undisputed home of British variety and light entertainment in the twentieth century.

Marsh was closely associated with Moss Empires, who controlled the Palladium from 1946 under the management of Val Parnell, who in turn brought the greatest American stars – Jack Benny, Judy Garland, Ethel Merman, Danny Kaye (who famously sat on the front of the stage dangling his legs in the orchestra pit), Bob Hope, Frank Sinatra – to Argyll Street. He also supervised ITV's *Sunday Night at the London Palladium*, Britain's most popular variety show, first broadcast in September 1955 starring Gracie Fields and Guy Mitchell. Tommy Trinder was the host, followed in due course by Bruce Forsyth, Norman ('Swinging') Vaughan, Larry ('Shut that door') Grayson and Jimmy Tarbuck.

As the credits rolled on *Sunday Night*, the cast of dancers, singers and stars would wave to the audience from a revolving stage as the orchestra played Cyril Ornadel's iconic theme music. That revolve, installed under the stage in the 1930s, is long gone, replaced by a 'double-doughnut' revolve device last used for the smash-hit revival of *Joseph and His Amazing Technicolor Dreamcoat* in 1991; the composer Andrew Lloyd Webber's company, Really Useful Theatre Group, now controls the Palladium, along with Drury Lane, the Adelphi and Her Majesty's.

The Palladium, designed by Frank Matcham as a large-scale variety house at a cost to the entrepreneur Walter Gibbons of £250,000 (perhaps £10 million in today's money), opened on Boxing Day 1910. It stands on the original site of the Duke of Argyll's house, which was built over an artesian well in 1650. By the mid-nineteenth century, this had fallen into disrepair, and morphed into a warehouse over the vaults and was later leased to the Corinthians Bazaar, an amusement arcade, and, in 1871, Hengler's Circus, which specialised in horses and kept its stables all around the ring, an equine incursion commemorated still in the colourful safety curtain. There was also an ice-skating rink in the 1880s.

The location of the new Tube at Oxford Circus was an important consideration for Gibbons. A flimsily printed programme of 1918 – proclaiming thrice-daily variety shows (comedians, singers, jugglers, ventriloquists, acrobats and a singing violinist) with advertisements for 'Black and White Scotch Whisky of Quality' and Fuller's Chocolates – boasts of the Palladium's status as the hub of the entertainment world by reason of this proximity 'whence underground Electric Trains radiate to all parts of London and the suburbs at intervals of a few minutes, whilst Omnibuses on all routes pass the theatre'.

There have been many structural and decorative alterations over the past twenty years, but Matcham's magnificent temple-like frontage remains, its portico and pediment, with statues aloft, seven first-floor bays and a grand three-door entrance up a short stairway; and his auditorium of two cantilevered tiers decorated in French rococo style is as warm and welcoming as ever, even with a seating capacity well in excess of 2,000. The foyer is a

*The exterior pediment of a famous variety house on Argyll Street, near Oxford Circus.*

handsome agglomeration of fibrous plaster, marble and brass, and you can still see the original safe where the manager locked up the box office takings. The current box office, housed to the left of the entrance, once resembled a railway station's ticket office within the building, with nine or ten wooden, windowed alcoves.

The Palladium was, in 1971, the first theatre to accept credit cards (Diners' Club only; American Express weren't interested) in response to the tourist trade; the show was a summer revue, *To See Such Fun*, starring Tommy Cooper, singer Anita Harris and pianist Russ Conway, with a group of Swedish comedy acrobats called, not at all misleadingly, The Stupids. They would not have been too much out of place on the opening programme in 1910, which was headlined by the eccentric music hall star Nellie Wallace. Tea was served in the Palm Court at the rear of the stalls, to the accompaniment of 'lady musicians in Pompadour gowns'. Box-to-box telephones were installed, and even an in-house hair-dressing salon. There were revues and pantomimes and, in 1930, the first Royal Variety Performance at the Palladium (the very first was at the Palace in 1912) in aid of the Entertainment Artists' Benevolent Fund, later the Variety Club.

After the demise of music hall, variety was resurrected in the 1930s with residencies of the Folies Bergère and the wildly popular Crazy Gang. Also, Peter Pan flew in every Christmas – Jean Forbes-Robertson, Nova Pilbeam, Elsa Lanchester (her husband, Charles Laughton, was Captain Hook) and Anna Neagle all played Peter. This history fills every nook and cranny in the place, though some garish pantomime scenes and portraits of male impersonator and pantomime principal boy Vesta 'Burlington Bertie' Tilley and George Robey ('the Prime Minister of Mirth') are painted and panelled over in the glorious Cinderella Bar at dress circle level; here, though, the smokers' original spittoon runs along the foot of the bar, itself removed from the side of the rococo-rich room to the front loggia side in the

*The view from the gods, the safety curtain showing the theatre in the days of horses and stables in Hengler's Circus.*

*The lounge of the star's dressing room.*

*The quick-change area under the stage.*

1950s. A Laura Knight painting of a lady in a box watching the Crazy Gang complements, on the opposite wall, a fine portrait of the actress known simply as 'June' (full name, June Howard Tripp), who played, doe-eyed and demure, opposite Ivor Novello in Alfred Hitchcock's early silent movie *The Lodger*. Hitchcock used the Palladium as a setting for his theatre scenes with the Memory Man at the start of *The Thirty-Nine Steps*.

The entrance to the Cinderella Bar is flanked by a bust of Bruce Forsyth donated by his son-in-law and a plaque, installed at a cheerily miffed Tommy Steele's insistence, in response to Brucie's bust, which records the highest number of Palladium appearances by a single artist – Steele himself – in exorbitantly long runs of *Hans Christian Andersen*, *Scrooge*, *Singin' in the Rain* and the venue's biggest-ever pantomime, *Dick Whittington* in 1970. The proportions of the house, and Matcham's great trick of combining width and shallowness, are best appreciated from the dress circle. The upper circle, too, is a homely place, boasting remnants of William Gibbons' 'bio box', which he installed to project photographs of Scott's Antarctic expedition as part of one of his first shows.

Other architectural oddities include a backstage 'donkey run' for live animals, leading from stage level directly onto Great Marlborough Street; the survival of little box office stations, now painted over, for customers to the pit and the gallery; the relocation of the much-missed 'square' bar in the Variety Bar (formerly the Palm Court) to the back wall, carried out to ease customer congestion; and the replacement of the rectangular, cosy Tudor Bar – where some riotously

enjoyable pre-lunch Press receptions were held by Louis Benjamin and Tony Wells in the 1960s and 1970s – with a set of much-needed ladies lavatories.

As in most Victorian and Edwardian theatres, the dressing rooms today are scant and underwhelming, though Yul Brynner demanded the installation of a jacuzzi and a gilded throne raised on a dais while playing in *The King and I* in 1979. Brynner was lionised by stage door fans during the run, but was brusque with most of them. One rebuffed lady admirer stalked him regularly with a bunch of flowers which he never acknowledged. One night, over-exasperated and driven to despair, she finally bashed him over the head with her floral arrangement; a unique instance, said one Moss Empires wag, of the fan hitting the shit.

*The King and I* was the first in a long sequence of musical theatre productions that seemed to proclaim the death of the variety stage era. It was followed in the 1980s by Michael Crawford in *Barnum*, Steele in *Singin' in the Rain* and George Hearn and Denis Quilley in *La Cage aux Folles*. But all of these shows contained elements of variety within them. The Palladium has a knack of renewing itself in the spirit of its own ineradicable traditions, and this wonderful, much-loved house reanimated another great strand in its extraordinary and colourful history by presenting its first lavish Christmas pantomime for twenty-nine years at the end of 2016.

London Palladium

8 Argyll Street, London W1F 7TE

www.reallyusefultheatres.co.uk

TOP LEFT *This preserved letterbox dates back to 1900: Moss Empires was Britain's biggest theatre chain, operating the Palladium from 1946.*

TOP RIGHT *The orchestra pit.* ABOVE *The performer's view from the stage.*

# London Coliseum

Built to invoke the wide range of spectacle in its Roman namesake – sea battles, gladiatorial combat, executions and scenes from classical mythology – Oswald Stoll's 1904 London Coliseum (known as the Coliseum Theatre 1931–68), designed by Frank Matcham, was intended as the last word in Edwardian variety theatre, the biggest palace of pleasure with the widest proscenium in town. Even though it has been home to English National Opera for over forty years, that is still very much how it appears.

Stoll had spent time watching the commuters and day-trippers from the Home Counties spilling out from the new Charing Cross station towards Trafalgar Square, and picked his spot accordingly. Matcham had to be clever to build something so ambitious, and large, on a site that was limited, in St Martin's Lane, a street full of slums, brothels, stables and pubs. The frontage is modest at ground level: a canopied entrance and four heavy wooden double doors with iron torches for door handles. But it moves attractively upwards with a blend of Ionic columns, balustrades and varied entablature, the main entrance part of the solid, imposing tower that has classical statuary representing art, music, literature and science, with a (once revolving, now fixed) illuminated globe perched like a cherry on top and operating as a beacon in the night sky. The globe is supported by eight ripped Roman slave boys sporting six-packs.

Matcham's masterstroke, in the space at his disposal, was to tilt the auditorium on an acute angle to the frontage, thus increasing the radial width of the interior while creating a sufficient shallowness in the auditorium to ensure a sort of intimacy. Stoll wanted the place to appeal to a family audience so had no qualms about unleashing two mixed programmes a day, each of them playing twice daily, starting at noon (then at 3 p.m., 6 p.m. and 9 p.m.) and boasting a roster of comedy jugglers, 'cantankerous' ponies, aerial

*The Roman-style auditorium is the biggest palace of pleasure in town.*

*This marble lion is said to have the facial features of Oswald Stoll.*

*The foyer ceiling of Roman mosaics and carousing Edwardian ladies.*

acrobatics, a full orchestra, the dance of a thousand veils and a grand musical finale, one such showing the Russians and the Japanese launching into the Battle of Port Arthur 'on the open sea' in early 1904; the theatre opened on Christmas Eve that year, exactly one week before Bertie Crewe's new Lyceum at the other end of the Strand. And in its first week of operation, 67,000 people passed through. There was a grand saloon, a tea room on every level – managed by Fuller's of Regent Street – a baronial smoking hall, a palm court orchestra at the terrace top level, confectionary stalls and an American bar, and an in-house telegram and telephone service. On opening night, the theatre claimed in the programme to be offering the social advantages of a Club, the comfort of a Café and 'the pleasantest family resort imaginable'.

The effect at the time must have been amazing. Matcham's interior remains a gob-smacker, not just in its architectural sweep of cantilevered balconies, bow-fronted boxes and profusion of marble and plasterwork throughout, but in the daringly kitsch juxtaposition of Edwardian grandeur and Roman decoration. The foyer combines both styles in a mosaic dome featuring loose-gowned early-twentieth-century carousing ladies and – a recurring motif in the house – a punctuating pattern of Roman vases and amphorae, or wine containers. Among the amphorae inside you see rectangular tablets bearing the legend SPQR (Senatus Populusque Romanus), the Roman emblem of government, and then – best viewed from the grand or upper circle – the proscenium arch flanked by large Roman coins, eagles, and chariots drawn by lions apparently taking off into the auditorium, despite the cool insouciance of the half-naked charioteers.

Metallic shields glint and lion faces grizzle on the walls, and one lion at the foot of the grand foyer stairs to the grand circle is said to replicate the features of Oswald Stoll himself. Across the foyer, Stoll placed a memorial statue to his mother, Adelaide, who worked for him all her life; Stoll was thirty-seven when he opened the Coliseum and he died aged seventy-five in 1942. Born in Australia, he had run theatres in Britain, starting in Liverpool, where he had emigrated with Adelaide, a theatre manager herself, after the death of his father. He had formed Moss Empires with the much older Edward Moss

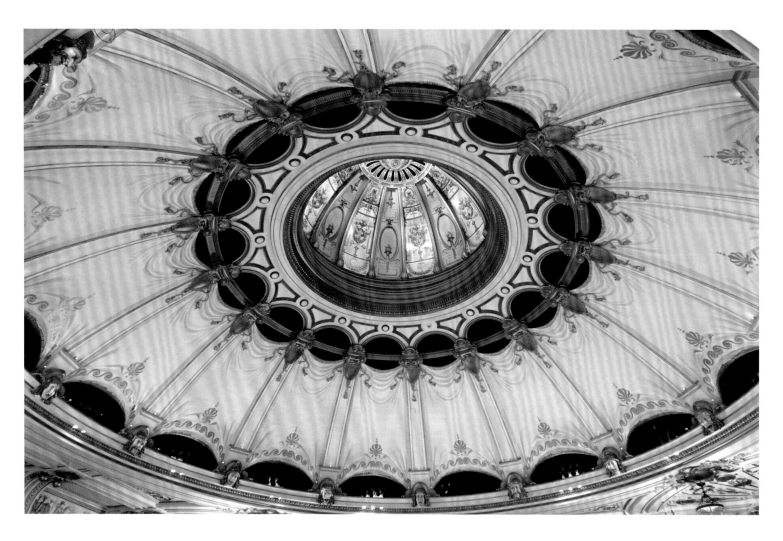

*The ceiling smoke outlet in the auditorium, a glass dome with canvas-like panels.*

in 1898, and the Coliseum is in some ways a monument to himself within a business partnership that dominated theatre ownership right through to the middle of the last century. But Stoll created with Matcham something that far transcended personal vanity. Functioning exclusively as an opera house since 1968 (with visiting ballet companies, Georgian dancers, Chinese acrobats and the like), it still retains its carnival and variety characteristics. Whereas the Royal Opera House has horseshoe snugness in its auditorium, the Coliseum has a gentler, wider crescent, and a magnificence unique in London theatre. It was also the first theatre in the country to be fitted with a revolving stage; this was a triple revolve, so that horses in the staging of the Derby, for instance, could gallop against the revolve while the scenery moved around them in the opposite direction. One of the jockeys was thrown against the proscenium and killed on the opening night.

Stoll had to be quick on his feet because the scope and range of his programming couldn't be maintained beyond the opening few seasons. But the theatre recovered from 1909 onwards, when variety legends such as Harry Lauder, Little

Tich and Vesta Tilley topped the bill, which often included great actors, too, such as Ellen Terry and Sarah Bernhardt. Diaghilev brought the Ballet Russes for seasons in 1918, 1924 and 1925. The Coliseum held the first public stage demonstration of television in July 1930; 'Truly,' moaned the renowned theatre historians, Mander and Mitchenson, 'the writing was on the wall!'

Not entirely, though, for the place became what we'd now recognise as a regular theatre in the very next year, 1931, with the spectacular presentation of the Berlin operetta *White Horse Inn*, which ran for two years, the Coliseum standing in for a fully realised Tyrolean village with a cast of 160 actors, three sets of bandsmen and a massive chorus. This set the seal on the Coliseum's future. More musicals followed and when Prince Littler succeeded Stoll (and the structure had survived two mild bombing scares during the war), he resumed business with a string of American musical theatre classics – *Annie Get Your Gun*, *Call Me Madam*, *Guys and Dolls*, *The Pajama Game*, *Bells Are Ringing*, and *The Most Happy Fella* – right through to 1960. In 1961, MGM took a long lease for the use of the theatre as a cinema: *Gone with the Wind* was followed by a short-lived era of Cinerama. In 1968, the Coliseum became the London home of the Sadler's Wells Opera after a short closure, complete redecoration and the construction of a large orchestra pit. The first production, *Don Giovanni*, was directed by John Gielgud who, at an early cast and chorus run-through with the orchestra in full flow in their splendid new cavern, rushed from the back of the stalls, unhappy with the groupings on the stage, and shrieked to the conductor, 'Stop, oh stop, that terrible music!' Sadler's Wells became the new English National Opera in 1974, and the ENO has struggled on, in good times and bad times, ever since.

A £41 million centenary restoration project in 2004, the freehold now held by ENO, saw the original burgundy colour scheme restored in the auditorium (it had gone blue and cream in the 1970s) and the bars and public areas renewed; the stalls bar seems to be registering an ongoing tussle between champagne bar exclusivity and airport lounge-style utilitarianism, almost a metaphor of the creative tensions in ENO's production schedule. Canvas-like panels all around the glass dome in the ceiling reinforce a sense of luxuriant heat in the auditorium, while the artists' canteen directly beneath the stage is spread around the white-painted axle of that spectacular revolve, which was removed just before the advent of Sadler's Wells Opera. The acoustics have always been superb. A good night out in this theatre is as good as any in London, not least because the house that Stoll and Matcham built retains its perfect blend of ornate grandeur and popular informality.

London Coliseum

St Martin's Lane, London WC2N 4ES

www.eno.org

*The view from the stage.*

# Dominion Theatre

Many London theatres doubled as cinemas for brief periods in the 1930s and 1940s, but only the gigantic Dominion, poised on the cusp of north London at Tottenham Court Road Tube station, was designed for dual purpose. Its location was key to Moss Empires when they commissioned a firm of architects who had built up a big business, some of it with them, in the north-east of England, just as the proximity of the new Oxford Street Underground station was an important factor in the location of the London Palladium.

The Dominion opened in 1929 with an all-American golf musical called *Follow Thru*, now remembered only, if at all, for the songs 'Button Up Your Overcoat' and 'My Lucky Star'. Since this inauspicious opening, its fortunes have been decidedly mixed, and it remains the case that whenever you enter the vast cinema-style foyer, you can never be entirely sure what to expect. Even fans of the long-running musical *We Will Rock You*, written by comedian Ben Elton around the songs of Queen – which defied an avalanche of critical disapproval when it opened in 2002 to run for twelve years – must have emerged confused by the show's inane narrative.

This is a theatre where the spectacular, and the unashamedly superficial, reign supreme. No surprise, really, given the provenance of the situation at St Giles Circus: a medieval leper hospital morphed into a brewery where, in 1814, a monster vat of porter exploded, killing eight people who thus drowned in their own sorrows. The brewery continued in business until 1922. Then a fairground dropped anchor and, in 1925, the site was levelled and screened around, opening as Luna Park in aid of the Middlesex Hospital reconstruction fund; a large tent offered three variety shows a day.

*The vast 1929 auditorium in a theatre designed for the dual purpose of stage spectaculars and cinema.*

*Lattice-like ironwork and lanterns in the upper foyer champagne bar area.*

The new Dominion's façade, an extraordinary blend of neoclassical and Art Deco, with a giant griffin on the roof, proclaimed a very modern sort of pleasure dome, with 3,000 seats (today, the capacity is 2,000), spacious circulation areas including a café overlooking the entrance, Chinese-looking pink lanterns and lots of ironwork that starts out front on the curved attic storey and works through in the metallic sheen of the lattice-like stairways and the balustraded balconies on the café (now an agreeable champagne bar). Mirrored walls suggest more intimate encounters until you enter the vastness of the auditorium. Soon after the place opened, some bars and outer rooms were removed and, in 1932, the Dominion was the first stop on a world tour of Charlie Chaplin's movie *City Lights* after its American premiere, and Chaplin made an appearance at the screening in the presence of King George V.

One of the hospitality rooms is named today for Chaplin and tells the story of the theatre since those early days in playbills, newspaper cuttings and industry reports. After a flurry of film stars – Maurice Chevalier, Sophie Tucker and Judy Garland – appeared on variety bills, the theatre was a cinema almost interruptedly for fifty years, punctuated by visits in the 1970s by Welsh National Opera, Georgian dancers and Chinese acrobats. In 1958, the upper circle was closed and a Todd-AO widescreen and projection box installed by the new owners, RKO, ushering in long runs of three major musical movies based on Broadway shows: *South Pacific* (1958–62), *West Side Story* (1962–5) and *The Sound of Music* (1965–73). Once again, new owners wrought radical changes when, in 1972, the stage was rebuilt and new dressing rooms added, shrugging off moves to redevelop the site.

The Dominion reverted to its 'live performance' self with *Time* in 1986, a spectacular multi-media musical about a rock

*The green room.*

*Large fly floor.*

star and his band transported to a court in the Andromeda Galaxy to justify themselves and preserve world peace. Laurence Olivier appeared, but only as a gigantic hologram, a god hatched from an over-sized egg, acting as mentor to the rock star, played by Cliff Richard. The *New York Times* set the sort of derisory critical tone that would bedevil several subsequent Dominion musicals: 'If present trends go on, John Napier [the designer] and his team will doubtless one day find themselves recreating the entire state of Iowa for a rock musical about the Little Red Hen, or reconstructing the Alps for one about Heidi; but until then *Time* can claim it has provided the most sensational contrast between mountainous spectacle and molehill content the musical theatregoer has seen.' The Dominion was under the cosh again in 1990, when demolition was mooted to make way for a hotel, but yet again a vociferous campaign prevailed, and the New York impresario James Nederlander bought half a stake in the business with Apollo Leisure. This signalled another upturn in the theatre's fortunes, with an extensive and sensitive refurbishment and two well-received big musical shows, *Grand Hotel* in 1992 and Disney's *Beauty and the Beast* in 1997.

The dominant colours in the auditorium were originally blue and silver, now succeeded by gold and burgundy. Apart from the metalwork, the decoration of roses and discs in the woodwork is carried right through the house, and in the carpets. The theatre was closed for over four months after *We Will Rock You* for new seating and carpeting, as well as repainting and the replacement of the Art Deco chandeliers and light fittings. There is a large and well-used rehearsal room above the foyer on the first floor, a huge hydraulic lift installed in 1997, and an orchestra pit. Five technical staff and two dozen other backstage and front-of-house staff are accommodated in offices in nearby Great Russell Street. The maintenance of a large theatre such as this is never-ending; a seemingly tedious and unimportant task such as replacing 1,500 bolts in the grid above the fly tower can only be done one by one, over several days, by someone not prone to vertigo. By a lucky chance, in 2014 the original griffin was discovered in a box, and is now restored to its rightful place on the top of the frontage.

Dominion Theatre
268–269 Tottenham Court Road, London W1T 7AQ
www.nederlander.co.uk

# Prince Edward Theatre

Better known as a variety hall and a cinema, and as the London Casino, for the first forty years of its life, the Prince Edward was in fact designed as a theatre for the presentation of spectacular musicals – its stage is the third largest in London behind those of Drury Lane and the Royal Opera – and the major revamp and refurbishment in the early 1990s revealed an Art Deco gem with a warm and inviting auditorium redecorated in the original colours of fuchsia and gold, fitted out with beautiful lamps and grilles and many other unusual and fascinating features.

It's a large and imposing red brick Italianate palazzo that squats confidently on the corner of Greek Street and Old Compton Street as if spirited from Shaftesbury Avenue towards the dens and denizens of what remains of old Soho. Two giant brass torches are bolted to the brick wall either side of the canopied entrance, which has five arched doorways. An indented third storey frontage offers the surprising farmhouse detail of seven pairs of green slatted window shutters. And now, on a summer's evening, you can stand on a decked and well-appointed terrace at the dress circle level, in a bar that opens to theatre-goers at 6 p.m., and survey the teeming Soho street scene below. The stage door round the back on Frith Street is dead opposite Ronnie Scott's Jazz Club and right next to the commemorated (blue plaque) site of the house where the infant prodigy Mozart lived and composed with his father for fifteen months in 1764. There's a legend engraved on the stone lintel identical to the one at the Palace Theatre: 'The World's greatest Artistes have passed and will pass through these doors.'

The theatre was built in 1930 – the first of four built in the West End that year – on the site of a former royal drapery. The

architect, Edward A. Stone, and the French interior designers, Marc-Henri Levy and Gaston Laverdet, had created the Piccadilly Theatre in 1928 and went straight on to do the Whitehall, another Grade II listed Art Deco theatre currently disguised as the more workaday, functional Trafalgar Studios with a single, steeply raked auditorium and a small black coffin of a studio theatre attached. The recovered joys of the Prince Edward are at least some compensation for that sacrilegious intervention. The opening show in 1930, framed in a proscenium arch of niches covered in Lalique amber glass, alas no more, was *Rio Rita*, the first Broadway musical to make a successful transition to the big screen. But it flopped in Old Compton Street. The Lord Chamberlain then demanded the removal of four lascivious female figures, each eighteen foot high, placed outside the theatre in 1932 to advertise the burlesque *Un Vent de Folie*; the producer protested that, while he admitted the cut-outs were indeed scantily clad, 'For my part, I can see nothing indecent in them.' Even Josephine Baker doing her banana dance in 1933 couldn't stir the theatre's fortunes as easily as she could the customers' libidos. The Prince Edward tottered until, in 1936, a syndicate, including the architect, took over and renamed it the London Casino, offering cabaret with dinner and the occasional variety show. A new apron stage for dancing was linked by wide stairs – the spectacular, forward-leaning loges (private boxes) are their legacy – to the balconies, a kitchen was installed under the stage and the stalls lounge became a cocktail bar. The waiters' rest rooms were upstairs behind the green shutters, where today sits an ice machine and other utilities.

The place closed on the outbreak of war but re-opened in 1942 as the Queensberry All-Services Club, broadcasting to

*Boxes, with drapery and one of the distinctive loges below on a wide staircase.*

*The star's dressing room.*

British forces overseas every Sunday afternoon, and staging a monthly boxing tournament to subsidise the visiting bands of Mantovani, Jack Hilton and Glenn Miller. There were games rooms, bathrooms, hairdressing salons and writing rooms. Vera Lynn lifted the nation's spirits and Petula Clark became an overnight child star in 1942 when she responded to a producer's request to settle the audience's nerves during an air raid. Bing Crosby sang through the whine of London's first flying bomb in 1944.

The producers Tom Arnold and Emile Littler re-opened for theatre business in the London Casino in 1946 with *Mother Goose*, shortly followed by Ivor Novello's *The Dancing Years*, which Arnold had been touring round the country for ten years since its Drury Lane premiere. Variety

alternated with ballet seasons and pantomimes and Robert Nesbitt presented three editions of his *Latin Quarter* revue before, in 1954, the renamed Casino Cinerama Theatre was, for the next twenty years, a movie house, with a 64-foot-wide screen, stereophonic sound, forty-eight loudspeakers and three synchronised projection boxes; some films – including the narrative epic *How the West Was Won* (1968) and Stanley Kubrick's sensational *2001: A Space Odyssey* – ran continuously for over a year.

But under Bernard Delfont's new ownership in 1974, live theatre returned and the Prince Edward reverted to its original name with the opening on a sun-bright summer evening of *Evita* by Tim Rice and Andrew Lloyd Webber. The show ran for eight years and established at last the

*The welcoming stalls bar with inlaid decoration and Art Deco fittings.*

destiny of the Prince Edward as a major musical theatre house: *Evita* star Elaine Paige subsequently appeared here in Rice and Abba's *Chess* and Cole Porter's *Anything Goes*. And when Cameron Mackintosh joined forces with Delfont, the three-month £3.5 million refurbishment period was declared complete with the opening of *Crazy For You* (1993), a Gershwin songbook directed by Mike Ockrent and choreographer Susan Stroman. Mackintosh has since played host to a five-year run of *Mamma Mia!* and a six-year run of *Jersey Boys* while producing two musical blockbusters with Disney – *Mary Poppins* and, most recently, *Aladdin* – the very same pantomime (home-grown version) that marked the end of the Prince Edward's first theatre phase in 1935.

The foyer is unusually circular, with a new Amadeus hospitality room to the side fitted out with tapestries, beautiful lamps and a big stone ashtray guarded by a miniature black and white marble leopard. The seating throughout is a racy purple on red carpeting. The circles have a drapery motif in the painted plasterwork (acknowledging the former occupancy of the site?) and there are ferns, fruit and flowers everywhere. Those ten distinctive loges, five on each side of the auditorium, seat two people in four of them, three in two, and another four in four, like graduating stepped boxes. The stalls bar downstairs has an enchanting photograph of the dancing girls in *Rio Rita* and another small hospitality side room named for Julie Andrews, the original Mary Poppins on film, of course, but also a young star of Prince Edward pantomimes; photographs on the wall show her (and her legs) in the title role of *Humpty Dumpty* in 1948 and as Princess Balroubadour in yet another *Aladdin* in 1951, four years before she became an overnight star in *The Boy Friend* on Broadway.

Dressing rooms and toilets are finished to an unusually high standard, decorated with striped green and grey wallpaper, just as the auditorium is fitted out with striking Art Deco grilles and lamps that, together with the plasterwork and the rectilinear coloured ceiling, suggest a setting of exotic, even Egyptian, lushness. And the latest glamorous touch has been to redecorate the bars in silver wallpaper; one has a caricature of Josephine Baker plus bananas, another a signed gift to Mackintosh (from the

prominent producer to the coach party trade of the 1960s and 1970s, Harold Fielding) of a poster commemorating the only London appearance, in this theatre in 1947, of the French music hall legend Mistinguett, at one time the highest paid female entertainer in the world. She was a bit shaky on her once heavily insured pins, apparently, but she was, by then, seventy-two. The Prince Edward, or the London Casino, must have seemed like a second natural home for her notoriously risqué Parisian routines.

Prince Edward Theatre
Old Compton Street, London W1D 4HS
www.princeedwardtheatre.co.uk

BELOW *A statue on the staircase to the dress circle.*

OPPOSITE, ABOVE AND BELOW *The auditorium, with purple seats and exotic lushness.*

# Lyceum Theatre

The Lyceum Theatre is the theatre of Henry Irving (1838–1905), our first theatrical knight and greatest stage star of the Victorian era; well, the portico and the frontage on Wellington Street, south of the Royal Opera House and glancing sideways across Waterloo Bridge, is certainly Irving's. He signed off as Shylock in 1902 but the sixth, and present, Lyceum was rebuilt two years later, designed by Bertie Crewe as an ornate music hall, and Irving never appeared in it.

It was that baroque decoration on the balconies – descried through the murk of an impromptu National Theatre performance of the medieval Mystery Plays lit by lanterns and braziers in 1985 – that prompted a *Daily Telegraph* theatre critic to proclaim 'a luscious old playhouse – fluted Tuscan pillars, curved out-swelling boxes, plaster figures of maidens and gods, and everywhere balustrades, urns, wrought iron, escutcheons, gilt and Pompeian red – all the long neglect of its Victorian heyday. Everyone asks, why can't it all be restored?'

Ten years later it was, and Disney's stage musical *The Lion King*, which opened in 1999, has been running ever since. But even by the volatile standards of London theatre's bricks and mortar history, the Lyceum's story is strangely bizarre. The first Lyceum, one hundred yards away on the Strand in 1772, was an exhibition room of paintings and sculpture, some of whose members defected to form the Royal Academy. It then came under the ownership of a tailor on the Strand, who let out the premises for concerts, lectures, and theatricals for unemployed actors entertaining each other. He also hosted the Beefsteak Club, founded by John Rich who had produced John Gay's *The Beggar's Opera* – the show that was said to have made Gay rich and Rich gay. Beefsteak rules prohibited the consumption of pickles until members had been stuffed with a third helping of rump steak washed down with porter, so it

*The auditorium of ornate plasterwork and Pompeian red.*

*The auditorium as viewed from the upper circle.*

was no surprise, perhaps, that Madame Tussaud showed her waxworks here for the first time in 1802. The Lyceum played host to the Drury Lane company after their theatre burned down in 1809; and the place, extensively rebuilt by Samuel Beazley in 1815, was the first London theatre to be lit by gas and, in 1817, the first to offer reduced prices at twice-nightly performances. The place was alight, and literally so, when it burned down in a fire of its own in 1830.

Beazley's second new Lyceum, built to the west of the old theatre in 1834, was the first in Britain to have a balcony projecting over the circle, and the first with an advance booking facility. It became known as the Royal Lyceum Theatre in 1843 and briefly as the Royal Italian Opera in 1856 when Covent Garden burned down and the singers decamped two hundred yards down the road to Wellington Street. Various managements had mixed success until one Hezekiah Bateman took the theatre as a showcase for his three daughters and engaged an unknown actor, Henry Irving, as his leading man. In 1871, Irving appeared in a melodrama, *The Bells*, as a haunted burgomaster whose nightmare

is unleashed by the intervention of a mesmerist. After a momentous and sensational first night, on the way home in a hansom cab, Irving's pregnant wife asked him if he was going to make a fool of himself like that all his life; he stopped the cab, got out, walked off, and never spoke to her again. By the time he played Hamlet in 1874, he was recognised as the greatest actor since Garrick and Kean, and his Shylock in 1879, with Ellen Terry an equally unprecedented Portia, acclaimed as his special triumph.

Irving took over the management of the theatre in 1878 with Terry his leading lady through his glory years of the 1880s, even as Shaw and the critic William Archer trumpeted the socialist, feminist theatre of Ibsen and Granville Barker that was looking to the future. After a fire in 1899, Irving sold on his control to a syndicate.

The competition for the new theatre from the Coliseum proved too much, and when the Melville Brothers took over in 1909, the programme of melodrama and pantomime widened to include opera and ballet. The theatre was sold for development and closed in 1939 with John Gielgud's fabled

*A candle-holding cherub on one of the boxes.*

*Hamlet*; in his curtain speech, Gielgud cried, 'Long live the Lyceum! Long live Ellen Terry! Long live Henry Irving!' The war interrupted plans to build a roundabout on this hallowed ground and for thirty years, from 1945 until it closed again in 1975, the Lyceum was London's best-known Mecca ballroom; the BBC transmitted episodes of the sedate and popular *Come Dancing* competition, precursor of its more raucous celebrity spin-off, *Strictly Come Dancing*. The 1980s was a decade of television events and live music, as well as *The Mysteries*, but when Apollo Leisure bought the Lyceum in 1994, they restored both the building and a sullied reputation in the West End.

Although Crewe's flamboyant plasterwork in the auditorium is currently damped down in matt red neutrality for *The Lion King*, the theatre had relaunched in 1996 as a fully up-and-running venue, plasterwork goldenly agleam, with a revival of *Jesus Christ Superstar*: naked *putti* on the balconies were still holding imaginary candles; the red, purple and gold ceiling hung like an exotic canopy over the stalls; the marble balustrades on each side of the royal circle were seen to their proper advantage; the key dates of 1834 and 1996

were emblazoned in gold on the frontage; and the names of Ellen Terry, Henry Irving and Irving's manager Bram Stoker – who wrote *Dracula* while in Irving's employ – engraved on the unprepossessing outer brick wall at the rear.

Two Broadway theatres are named for critics – the Brooks Atkinson and the Walter Kerr – but the closest London has come is to have an impish portrait of Jack Tinker, the much-loved critic of the *Daily Mail* who died in 1996, in a small champagne bar in the Lyceum stalls, though 'Jack's Corner' is currently used as a storage area. Since the theatre came into the ownership of the Ambassador Theatre Group, the main foyer has been redecorated in green, grey and gold, the royal circle 'ballroom' bar made over in metallic, veiny wallpaper panels and a large 'Ambassador Lounge' for VIP guests and private functions fitted out with stripy sofas, comfy cushions and a small bagel-making kitchen.

Lyceum Theatre
21 Wellington Street, London WC2E 7RQ
www.lyceum-theatre.co.uk

# Prince of Wales Theatre

Stepping into the Prince of Wales is like climbing aboard an ocean-going liner. And that was the idea behind Robert Cromie's spectacular Art Deco 1937 theatre, which opened with *Les Folies de Paris*, a non-stop revue playing from 2 p.m. to 11 p.m. The previous theatre on the site, the Prince's, was home to French revue, too, as well as the first English musical comedies. And the history and style of both theatres are embroiled in the inventive and stylish 2004 refurbishment by Renton Howard Wood Levin architects for Delfont Mackintosh Theatres.

The original Prince's, a traditional three-tier theatre, was designed in 1884 by C.J. Phipps and renamed the Prince of Wales in 1886. While Gilbert and Sullivan were busy writing comic operas, the impresario George Edwardes was launching the first native musical comedies, *In Town* (1892) and *A Gaiety Girl* (1893), which took a light-hearted spin on backstage and society intrigue, the second of them with bathing beauties and fantastical costumes; these shows attracted the first 'Stage Door Johnnies': flâneurs and financiers on the hunt for glamorous wives. Marie Tempest played Nell Gwyn in 1900 – the costume designs are on display in the theatre today – Ivor Novello had his first play, *The Rat* (1924), produced here, and Beatrice Lillie, Gertrude Lawrence and Jack Buchanan appeared in the André Charlot revues of the 1920s. But the theatre's many corridors and smoking rooms limited the seating capacity, so the profits gained paid for a new theatre and enlarged stage promising an even greater box office return.

Gracie Fields laid the new theatre's foundation stone, which is lodged in the wall near ground level on Oxenden Street. Cromie brought the circle level to within 21 feet of the stage and just 11 feet above the stalls, enlarging the old theatre's outer dimensions. The exterior was made in artificial white stone.

*The auditorium from the stage.*

*View into the orchestra pit.*

A high cylindrical tower facing towards Piccadilly Circus and Shaftesbury Avenue contained the air-conditioning plant and boiler house. There were further modifications made to the auditorium in the 1960s, but nothing so drastic or dramatic as the DMT renovation, which re-imagined Cromie's part-realised Art Deco plans with a vengeance throughout the building. A superb glass model of Cromie's design in the new foyer makes it clear that this was intended as a streamlined ship of dreams and edification comparable only to the much grander Broadcasting House of 1932.

The great comedian Sid Field made his first and last appearances in the Prince of Wales. He died in 1950 during the run of *Harvey* by Mary Chase, in which he played Elwood P. Dowd, an alcoholic haunted by a six-foot imaginary white rabbit (James Stewart made the movie and returned in the same role to this same theatre in 1975); the programme for the 1949 production, which also starred Athene Seyler, has a mouth-watering guide to what else is playing in the West End: Peter Brook's production of *Dark of the Moon*, *Annie Get*

*Your Gun* at the Coliseum, *Oklahoma!* at Drury Lane, *The Beaux Stratagem*, Terence Rattigan's *Adventure Story*, Peggy Ashcroft in *The Heiress*, Edith Evans in James Bridie's *Daphne Laureola*, and so on . . . The 1950s saw more revue at the Prince of Wales, with the likes of Terry-Thomas, Peter Sellers and Norman Wisdom, and Josh Logan's *The World of Suzie Wong*, a musical which prompted Kenneth Tynan to refer to a subsequent Rodgers and Hammerstein show as 'a world of woozy song'.

In the 1960s, this was a big musical house – *Funny Girl* with Barbra Streisand making her only London appearance in a stage role, for just a few months, in 1966, Juliet Prowse in *Sweet Charity*, *Promises Promises* by Burt Bacharach and Neil Simon. The Royal Variety Performance of November 1963 was notable for a set by the Beatles in their breakthrough year. Introducing their third and last number ('Twist and Shout'), John Lennon said, 'I'd like to ask your help. Will the people in the cheaper seats clap your hands? And for the rest of you, if you'll just rattle your jewellery . . .' The ever-sporting Queen Mother smiled and waved discreetly back to the stage.

*Noël Coward's Steinway piano from his home in Les Avants.*

*A bust of Noël Coward by Clemence Dane.*

The new theatre was, and is, a cavern of renovated Art Deco delights, gleaming with chrome, brass, zinc and fluted glass work. Portholes, circular mirrors, polished rails and curved walkways everywhere. The signage uses a 1930s typeface known as Odessa. Downstairs, the Delfont Room, the main stalls bar, has been stripped of its collection of old-style theatre bills – distributed elsewhere on the stairways, the majority archived – and redecorated with posters and art works more suited to the Art Deco ceiling, dance floor, lighting and long bar with its frontage of small, square glass blocks in four units of three dozen each. This bar now has fourteen new ladies' toilets, the walls painted shocking pink, with a Barbra Streisand poster, and an accessible facility papered with a large wallpaper print of the old Prince's Theatre.

Next door, and up a few stairs, is the Piano Room, decorated with Erté prints, a bust of Noël Coward by the playwright Clemence Dane, and a 'practical' public pay phone glowing blue. The piano is Coward's Steinway from his house in Les Avants, Switzerland. En route to the American Bar at dress circle level is a small overflow area, Les Folies, taking you straight into the rotunda, looking up into the tower which is blocked off with a witty 'double aspect' painting by Francis Hamel: from one side you see the tower, from the other, a ship that could be the theatre.

The auditorium has new seats and carpeting in umber red, brass rails, and some distinctive acoustic panels at the sides and back which are wooden and painted in a metallic matt gold that reproduces a feature of Cromie's original design of panelling in figured walnut. The stage itself is fairly shallow, and the wing space limited. But of all London theatres, this may well be the one most worth exploring without the diversion of an actual performance. It's quite stunning, and the best sort of living shrine to an art form, and a decorative style.

Prince of Wales Theatre

Coventry Street, London W1D 6AS

www.princeofwalestheatrelondon.info

POPULAR LANDMARKS

# Shakespeare's Globe

Shakespeare's Globe, an oaken-framed theoretical replica of the wooden 'O' where audiences first saw *Hamlet*, *King Lear* and *Henry V*, opened in 1997, built in twenty curved bays of three galleries with a thatched roof, about 250 yards from the site of the original Globe right by the River Thames. It is now a fixed landmark on the South Bank together with its near neighbour the Tate Modern art gallery and, further along the river, the London Eye, the National Theatre and the Royal Festival Hall.

Not only that, but it is also arguably the most popular theatre in London, not remotely the 'heritage-style' tourist-baiting theme park (though tourists certainly make a bee-line for the place) the cynics and most critics expected to see evolving, packed to the gills on afternoons and evenings between May and October, with seating on pine benches for 900 spectators and room in the yard for 700 'groundlings' paying £5 (an unchanged ticket price) for the privilege of being harangued by actors and pestered by the volunteer ushers when they flop to the floor. And with the Royal Shakespeare Company rarely, or less frequently, appearing in London, and the Open Air Regent's Park broadening its repertoire beyond the Bard, the Globe is now established as the undisputed top Shakespeare destination in the capital.

The theatre is at the beating heart of an International Shakespeare Centre, which delivers bespoke educational programmes for students and teachers worldwide. It involves the local community, and runs a superb on-site exhibition and tour programme. In 2014, the Globe opened an enchanting indoor candlelit theatre on the same site: the Sam Wanamaker Playhouse, designed to drawings discovered in 1969 in Worcester College, Oxford, and first thought to be those of Inigo Jones (now attributed to Jones's student, John Webb), with seating for 350 in a cockpit presenting a Jacobean and Elizabethan repertoire, baroque opera, solo shows, poetry and other musical events.

Sam Wanamaker, who died in 1993, was an American actor who campaigned for a Shakespearean modern-day Globe for many years. He'd been shocked to discover, on arriving in London in 1949, that there was no memorial to Shakespeare on Bankside beyond a stone and metal plaque on a brewery wall. That plaque – showing a bust of Shakespeare against a long-shot in relief of the Bankside Thames – is now at the site of the first Globe in Park Street (formerly Maiden Lane). That Globe was built in 1598 and burned down in 1613 when, during a performance of *Henry VIII*, a cannon was fired in the roof and sparked a blaze; no one died, though one groundling was injured, according to a contemporary report: 'his breeches on fire that perhaps would have broyled him if he had not, with the benefit of a provident wit, put it out with bottle ale'. The Globe – still open to the sky – was rebuilt with a tiled roof, but was closed down by the Puritans in 1642, along with all the other theatres, and demolished in 1644.

Wanamaker set up the Globe Playhouse Trust in 1970, battled with the local council, and gradually won over sponsors and investors on both sides of the Atlantic, as well as the theatrical and academic professions here. His architect Theo Crosby (who also died, in 1994, before the Globe opened) designed the timber frame which was made in five batches of four units, the joints of mortise (timber with a hole) and tenon (timber with a tongue of wood fitting into that hole) locked

PREVIOUS PAGE *Shakespeare's modern-day Globe has the galleried interior, thrust stage, tiring house and thatched roof of a famous 1596 sketch of the nearby Swan.*
OPPOSITE *The stage canopy of the heavens with a golden sunburst.*

*View from the gentlemen's rooms, decorated with scenes from mythology.*

*The theatre sits by the Thames on the South Bank.*

tight with oak pegs. Thousands of Tudor-style iron nails fixed floorboards to joists. Some of the most difficult decisions attached to questions about the size of the stage, how big a suitable roof for that stage, and where should the pillars go?

In the end, following suggestions in Johannes de Witt's famous sketch of the nearby Swan in 1596 (there is no evidence from the original Globe), they created a large rectangular thrust stage with a canopy of the heavens – a golden sunburst surrounded by signs of the zodiac – supported on two oaken pillars (painted in marble veneer and decorated with gold leaf) that were carefully positioned, after consultation with actors and directors, a minstrels' gallery and a 'tiring house' upstage with three entrances. The thatched roof – the first in London since the Great Fire of 1666 – was woven from water reed and fitted, at the insistence of Health and Safety officers, with sprinkler devices at every metre along its summit. A gabled attic houses stage machinery, a bell and a (non-inflammatory) cannon for battle scenes. A recent addition has been the painting of the four stage boxes at first gallery level, the so-called 'gentlemen's rooms', with scenes from classical mythology in a plan based on designs in other surviving Elizabethan and Jacobean buildings.

With the design in progress, there happened to be two important excavations in 1989: one at the original Globe which revealed little beyond the probable shape and dimensions of the outer walls, with chalk and brick foundations 6 feet deep; and the other, 150 feet further along Park Street, at the site of the Rose, the first theatre on the South Bank in 1587, and host to Christopher Marlowe's plays and Shakespeare's

enormously popular prentice pieces, the *Henry VI* trilogy and the savage blood bath *Titus Andronicus*. The Rose remains, a murky grey area you can still visit, are strangely unexciting. You have to think quite hard about how important this ground-floor site actually is, dankly preserved beneath an office block and revealing, just about, an octagonal outline of a much smaller theatre and its watery foundations. There are occasional performances on the cramped viewing platform.

Crosby's Globe designs began to be realised when a public appeal yielded sufficient money. 2,500 flagstones surround the theatre, each sold at a cost of £300 to celebrities, actors and supporters whose names are inscribed on them. The stroke of genius was to make an unexpected appointment of a brilliant actor, Mark Rylance, whose determination to investigate 'authentic' practice in music and staging was informed by a muscular, contemporary sensitivity, and a sort of crowd-pleasing but minimally coy method of communication, every show, the lightest comedy or darkest tragedy, ending with a company jig that sealed the deal with the audience. Rylance led for ten years by example, showing how to play intimately and naturally to a large house, experimenting with gender swaps – women were played by boys in Shakespeare's day and his writing is suffused with gusty sexual innuendo and a sort of amphibian ambiguity – but Rylance further complicated the sexual reverberations by having Vanessa Redgrave play Prospero in *The Tempest*, or an all-female cast play *The Taming of the Shrew*. He himself played Olivia in *Twelfth Night*, Cleopatra, Hamlet and Richard III to critical acclaim, and directed the company

TOP *An audience of 900 is seated in pine benches. The pit has room for a further 700 standing.*

ABOVE *The Globe has confounded all predictions of being a 'heritage centre' to become the most popular theatre in London.*

overall, and in specific productions, in each of his ten seasons in charge.

His successor in 2007, Dominic Dromgoole, was a director who continued to attract fine actors and mixed in more contemporary plays, often successfully achieving an epic, or 'public', dimension. Boldly, he sought no hiding place from Rylance's standards and reputation, but pushed on further, continuing experiments in Elizabethan practice and reconfiguring the audience's relationship with the stage. In 2012, he presented all thirty-seven Shakespeare plays in different languages from all over the world: *Romeo and Juliet* from Brazil, a Chicagoan hip-hop *Othello* and a Russian *Measure for Measure*. In 2014, as the Sam Wanamaker neared completion – an oaken bauble with two horseshoe galleries, elegant pillars and steel chandeliers hanging from a painted ceiling of blue sky, clouds and plump little *putti* – a world tour of *Hamlet* left the Globe, returning two years later after visiting 197 countries.

Dromgoole was succeeded in 2016 by Emma Rice of the renowned Cornish touring company Kneehigh, and she felt no qualms about immediately challenging the architecture, 'shared light' and unadulterated spoken word tradition of the place. Her opening production, *A Midsummer Night's Dream*, was heavily 'miked' and the auditorium invaded by a permanent installation of huge white balloons and long silken green tubes of forest foliage. Her contract was not renewed beyond 2018. Meanwhile, the Globe is expanding its work into China as part of the government's trade policy and has launched 'Project Prospero', a major capital investment and the final stage in realising Wanamaker's vision: a new building on the current site will comprise the library, production facilities, rehearsal and education studios and a new exhibition.

Shakespeare's Globe

21 New Globe Walk, London SE1 9DT

www.shakespearesglobe.com

*The candle-lit Sam Wanamaker Playhouse, with seating for 350, is designed from drawings discovered in Worcester College, Oxford, in 1969.*

# Sadler's Wells Theatre

Sadler's Wells, built above a seventeenth-century spring of allegedly healing water in Clerkenwell Priory, is the only London theatre to make itself the subject of one of its own productions. In 2016, the performer-free performance *No Body* gave us a dramatic light show on the stage which climaxed in the terrifying descent of an entire rig laden with 130 lamps, and included a tour of the rehearsal studios, wig and wardrobe rooms, and a couple of films showing a naked woman running through the city and a muscularly writhing, sweaty corps-de-very-modern-ballet. This was entirely in keeping with the Wells' history and status as an innovative force in our popular culture, the north London complement to the Old Vic; the Wells and the Vic are twin nurseries of our National Theatre, English National Opera and Royal Ballet. It all started in 1718, when Thomas Sadler, a canny developer and entrepreneur, created a Restoration 'leisure centre' for travellers and locals, also known as a bawdy 'musick house', well away from the censorship and patenting controls of the metropolis. The first stone theatre was built in 1765, and for thirty years from 1788, arguably the greatest British clown of all time, Joseph Grimaldi, prefigured music hall, pantomime and modern comedy with his peculiar, robust possession of the Italian harlequinade; exhausted, he discarded his cap and bells for the last time in 1828, aged just forty-seven, in a farewell speech from the stage: 'I now stand worse on my legs than I used to on my head.'

On the abolition of the patent monopoly on 'serious' drama in 1843, the actor-manager Samuel Phelps, a key figure in the continuity of our stage history, and of Shakespeare in performance, was able to produce all of Shakespeare's plays in an astonishing eighteen-year period. *Antony and Cleopatra* in 1849 was the play's first staging for a century, and that of

*The new auditorium offers perfect views of the stage from every seat in the house.*

ABOVE *The front-of-house is an architectural marvel of steel, chrome, wood and glass on four levels.*
OPPOSITE ABOVE *Leslie Edwards, Michael Somes and Margot Fonteyn.* OPPOSITE BELOW *The brick Sadler's Wells well in the stalls corridor.*

the beguiling romance and travelogue *Pericles* in 1854 the first since the Restoration. The Wells, redesigned by C.J. Phipps, with a capacity of 2,500, was now established as a significant playhouse. But when Phelps retired in 1862, the venue, redesigned by Bertie Crewe, reverted to music hall, with spells as a boxing venue and a skating rink. Briefly doubling as a cinema, it declined and closed in 1906, lying disused until an appeal was launched by Lilian Baylis and Reginald Rowe in 1927. With the help of the Carnegie Trust and Finsbury Borough Council, the theatre was acquired as a charity, rebuilt and re-opened by Baylis as a north London counterpart to the Old Vic in 1931.

The new building was described in *The Times* as 'an impressive composition of masses in brick, with a Georgian flavour', with a canopy over the principal entrance. At first, the acting company led by John Gielgud and Ralph Richardson alternated between the Wells and the Vic, but this arrangement ceased in 1934 and the Wells concentrated completely on opera and ballet. The Sadler's Wells Ballet created by Ninette de Valois evolved, after the war, into the Royal Ballet while the opera programme led directly to the formation of English National Opera at the Coliseum in 1968; that new dawn was heralded by the opening of Benjamin Britten's *Peter Grimes* at the Wells in 1945. Subsequent developments in choreography in Europe and America came to redefine the Wells as a creative

*The fly floor is operated by the world's first fully computerised system.*

centre of dance, and London's leading dance showcase. This identity was only achieved after a great struggle for survival when the original dance and opera companies moved on, and the building of what is, in effect, a brand new theatre at the end of the 1990s under the visionary stewardship of the producer and chief executive, Ian Albery, scion of the West End dynasty. The stage had been enlarged in 1938, the acoustics improved in 1959 and the proscenium arch redesigned. But nothing so drastic had ever been broached as this spectacular redesign by Renton Howard Wood Levin in 1999, a new London theatre for the new millennium and the first to be substantially funded by the National Lottery.

A new glass frontage reveals foyer areas on four levels, with stairways, bars, chrome banisters and light-coloured wooden floors. Running from top to bottom, just inside the entrance, are portraits of the sixteen associate artists who include Matthew Bourne, the Ballet Boyz and Sylvie

Guillem. The old Wells of sagging seats, plush red velvet and sandwiches in the bars – no other theatre served cheese and beetroot between bread slices – is replaced with a sleek, European ambience, ushers in black uniforms, and a permanent air of civilised festivity enhanced with the fairy lights twinkling in trees across the road all year. The house red is Portuguese. There is no longer a centre aisle, and no restricted view from any of the 1,500 seats, which are slightly raked in the stalls and which rise more steeply in the two cantilevered balconies to the top, where the old demarcation line with the gallery is obliterated. The Lilian Baylis studio, with blue seating for 200, previously accessed through the large scene-loading area and stage door on Rosebery Avenue, is opened out to the side, and there is a good new café with increased circulation areas for both artists and audiences.

The main stage has the first totally computerised flying system in the world and the new theatre is also the first to

*The orchestra pit lift below the stage.*

deploy its own ground water in the air-conditioning system, a nice nod to the original priory spring, whose deep brick well is preserved in the stalls corridor; until recently you could throw coins in there. Some of the theatre's original brickwork is revealed, bound in steel rivets, in square glass boxes like exhibits in a museum. There is living history, too, in the portraits of an unrecognisable Ian Albery and an unmistakable Alicia Markova, Britain's first prima ballerina, by the new café, alongside sculptured busts of alumni including Michael Somes and Margot Fonteyn, and two striking stone effigies of Comedy and Tragedy reproduced from a Matcham theatre elsewhere. While it is true that some of the old populist rough-and-tumble feel of the Wells has gone, the new premises are clearly aimed at the Islington in-crowd and the niche modern dance audience. The size of that niche is what counts, though; dance audiences are the main growth area in contemporary theatre. Peggy Ashcroft once said that a theatre either has an atmosphere or it

doesn't; it's not a quality for which you can plan or legislate. The new Wells has that atmosphere of buzz and excitement about it, and not just because there are plenty of clues to its significant history around the place. These clues also line the walls of the two nearby hostelries: the Shakespeare's Head, which has been in the management of the same family for over thirty years, and the 'newer' Wellsian Harlequin, a free house with obvious connotations of Grimaldi. Their posters and playbills attest not only to the spirit of the theatre but also to that of the audiences down the decades.

Sadler's Wells Theatre
Rosebery Avenue, London EC1R 4TN
www.sadlerswells.com

# The Old Vic

The Old Vic, which opened as the Royal Coburg in 1818 on the south side of the newly constructed Waterloo Bridge, is one of the oldest and most important theatres in London, seedbed and first home of our National Theatre, sprouting and surviving precariously across two centuries, and currently restored to something like its 1833 classical look, on its façade and in the auditorium, at least. Its roots are in the local rough house traditions of melodrama and music hall, and our modern Shakespearean history derives from two heroic presentations of the complete First Folio in 1914–23 and again in 1953–58. When Edmund Kean played Richard III and Othello here in 1831, he met with the full force of a rowdy, vibrant audience: 'I have never acted to such a set of ignorant, unmitigated brutes as I see before me,' he told them; over a century later, the audience knew better, and Laurence Olivier, Kean's ultimate successor, played both roles himself for the Vic, to more rapturous a welcome, the first during a famous 1944 wartime season at the New (now the Noël Coward; the Old Vic had been bombed), the second in his later pomp as the National's first artistic director on the Waterloo Road.

The Royal Coburg's foundation stone, now embedded on the Webber Road side, was laid by our royal family's ducal antecedents, Prince Leopold of Saxe-Coburg and Princess Charlotte of Wales – or, at least, by their 'proxy', an Alderman Samuel Goodbehere; presumably he said that, though the royals couldn't turn up, he 'could-be-here' – and announced a house of melodrama for an audience of over 4,000; its 'looking glass' stage curtain of sixty-odd pieces became one of the sights of London before it was removed as the roof was not strong enough to hold it. The theatre was redecorated and renamed the Royal Victoria

*The Old Vic is seedbed and first home of our National Theatre, now commercially operated by a non-profit trust.*

in 1834, the broken pediment at the top of the frontage showing a royal crest flanked by small figures of a lion and a unicorn. Six plain pillars support the canopy, with five tall sashed and arched windows at what is now dress circle bar level. A 'fourpenny gallery' of rudimentary benches was introduced in 1845, the scene in 1858 of an in-house disaster when a false fire alarm prompted a stampede killing sixteen people. Although the auditorium was redesigned with two tiers (its long-lasting configuration) in 1869 by J.T. Robinson, Frank Matcham's father-in-law, things went from bad to worse. The theatre was sold by auction, then sold again, and finally closed in 1880. In the same year, the Royal Victoria was leased to Emma Cons, a social reformer and first lady member of the London County Council; she is thrice memorialised – in a scrolled, now illegible, stone tablet on the Waterloo Road corner of the building, on a bronze plaque inside, and in the scruffy garden square on the other side of the Cut, favoured residence of winos and rats.

It was this disreputable air about the place – the theatre was known as 'a sink of iniquity' – that Cons countered by renaming it the Royal Victoria Hall and Coffee Tavern, the area we now know as the foyer fitted out with tables and chairs, the unchanged auditorium stiff with improving lectures and concerts. In 1888, Cons was compelled, in straitened circumstances, to form a charity which bought the freehold; further relief came with the textile manufacturer Samuel Morley making a big donation in 1894 and founding an adult education centre, Morley College, at the back of the building (where it stayed until 1923). In 1898, Cons summoned her niece, Lilian Baylis, who was teaching music in South Africa, to join her as assistant manager and, in 1912, when Cons died and Baylis took over, a legend, and the modern British theatre, was born.

Baylis, a do-gooding spinster like her aunt, was a bespectacled Cockney with a brusque manner and a lopsided visage who fried up her sausages on a small gas ring in the wings and prayed to God for support: 'Please send me a good actor, but send him cheap.' In 1914 she instigated the Old Vic Shakespeare Company in that historic First Folio season produced by Ben Greet and Robert Atkins. The company was led by Sybil Thorndike. She later hired such promising unknowns as Peggy Ashcroft, Ralph Richardson, Gielgud and Olivier. A young Mary Kerridge came to audition in the 1930s and Baylis was told there was a Miss Kerridge on the stage: 'Well, clear it up quickly and get on with the auditions,' she huffed irately. For five years from 1931, Baylis managed both the Old Vic and Sadler's Wells, shuffling a ground-breaking popular programme of

Shakespeare, ballet and opera between the two venues; a complete four-act set for *La traviata* slipped off a transport lorry and disappeared over Blackfriars Bridge. By 1935, the ballet and opera were based exclusively at the Wells. Baylis died in 1937, the Vic closed at the outbreak of war, and was bombed in 1941. The Old Vic School was founded in the wrecked theatre in 1947, moved on to Dulwich in 1950, when the renovated theatre re-opened, and thence to Bristol, where the theatre and new drama school in that city borrowed the Old Vic label. The Old Vic annexe, now modified and modernised as the National Theatre studio, opened on the corner of the Cut and Webber Street in 1958.

Michael Benthall produced the second First Folio season, and the last five seasons before the advent of the National in 1963 were directed by Tyrone Guthrie and Michael Elliott. The gung-ho, raffish style of the place was maintained by Richard Burton's crowd-pulling performances as Hamlet and Henry V in 1953 and 1955; in 1956, Burton and his matinée idol co-star, John Neville, alternated as Othello and Iago, their rival claques of supporters queuing separately round the theatre. At one performance, when drunk, they both went on as Othello, but nobody noticed, claimed Neville. In the last Old Vic Company season, in 1962, Burton returned with Elizabeth Taylor to see an old friend, Wilfrid

Lawson, in *Peer Gynt*. Lawson played the Button Moulder, who doesn't figure till the fifth act. So he sat with Burton and Taylor in the circle throughout the first four. Their heroic drinking before the show and during the intervals compensated for the entire Cons/Baylis era of temperance. Half-way through the fifth act, Lawson, who'd forgotten where he was, leant across to Burton and said, 'Look at this, this is where I come on . . .' and waited for himself to appear on the stage below.

Olivier led the National at the Old Vic for ten glorious years – his company included Michael Redgrave, Maggie Smith, Robert Stephens, Colin Blakely, Edith Evans, Derek Jacobi, Albert Finney – but was replaced by Peter Hall in readiness for the move to the South Bank in 1973. Extensive alterations included a new apron stage, a new proscenium, and the removal of the stage boxes by the iconoclastic designer Sean Kenny. The end of the 1970s saw a troop of visiting companies and an attempt by the Cambridge-based touring set-up Prospect Theatre to establish themselves as the new Old Vic company. This imploded badly when Peter O'Toole – who had opened Olivier's regime with a disappointing *Hamlet* – bombed in a sold-out but risible 1980 production of *Macbeth*. The Arts Council withdrew their support for Prospect and the company went into liquidation. The governors sold the freehold to discharge their debts and, after ninety-four years, the Vic returned to private ownership after inviting sealed bids. Andrew Lloyd Webber had lodged a bid of £500,000, hoping to create a forcing house for new British musicals, but was pipped at the post by a last-minute entry of £550,000 by the Canadian philanthropist, entrepreneur and discount store mogul 'Honest' Ed Mirvish. Ed's son, David, was the main man in the subsequent era, supervising extensive refurbishment and employing the brilliant maverick Jonathan Miller to produce seventeen shows across three years (1987 to 1990) before selling up in 1998 after a couple of years of Peter Hall being in charge.

With the architects Renton Howard Wood Levin, the Mirvishes restored not only the façade, but also the Robinson auditorium in its gold, cream and grey colour scheme, the boxes in three tiers of two on either side of the proscenium, redecorating the two handsome lyre-shaped balconies and re-upholstering the seats, raising the capacity to over 1,000. The foyer spaces were drastically remodelled and one single staircase created, rising from ground level through the dress and upper circles, with the box office repositioned to one side of the foyer. Not only that: the stage door on Waterloo Road was moved across to Webber Street, and new offices and wardrobe, with the rehearsal room, established more comfortably in the old Morley College wing. When the Mirvishes moved out, it was rumoured that the place might become a themed pub or even a lap-dancing club. At the last minute, a non-profit trust was formed involving the director Stephen Daldry, producer Sally Greene and Kevin Spacey, who had appeared at the Vic in an Almeida Theatre transfer of *The Iceman Cometh* by Eugene O'Neill in 1998. Elton John became chairman of the trust in 2002. In the following year, Kevin Spacey began an eleven-year stint as artistic director, combining this job with his Hollywood and television career in America. Matthew Warchus succeeded Spacey in 2015.

The theatre has seen an ongoing process of 'refreshment' since Sally Greene took over with Spacey. She has initiated a series of modern decorative adjustments that are not obviously theatrical. A red neon sign in the foyer reprises a favourite apothegm of Baylis, 'Dare always dare,' (as it happens, neon was discovered in 1898, the year Emma Cons arrived at the theatre) while a tree of lightbulbs rises like an art gallery installation through the staircase. The downstairs Pit Bar has been rechristened the Penny, and has a glass door and entrance punched into the wall on the Waterloo Road side proclaiming an 'artisan café and late-night bar' (open from 8 a.m. to 1 a.m.). The upstairs bars have wooden floors and no soft furnishings, so their airiness is curiously matched by their noisiness when full. Photographs of the Old Vic greats – Burton, O'Toole, Robert Helpmann, Olivier, Richardson, Gielgud and Spacey – have been removed to the third level stairway, en route to the Baylis bar, so as not to distract from a minimalist white interior design.

The Mirvishes restored the Robinson proscenium, but Greene and Spacey took all the seats out – on a temporary basis – and reconfigured the entire auditorium as an 'in-the-round' venue for revivals of Alan Ayckbourn's *The Norman Conquests* (directed by Matthew Warchus), Brian Friel's *Dancing at Lughnasa* and Cole Porter's *High Society*, the 'new' stalls rising in a bank to the dress circle level and a 'clubby' pop-up bar with sofas plonked in the rear stalls area under the back of the dress circle. There have even been shows performed with an audience of about 200 on the stage itself, the stage iron brought in to cut out the auditorium. The building, having proved its flexibility, will surely reassert itself. The four boxes nearest the stage are still named after Robert Atkins, Guthrie, Olivier and Michael Benthall.

The Old Vic

The Cut, London SE1 8NB

www.oldvictheatre.com

*The original rehearsal room at the top of the building in the old Morley College wing.*

# Royal National Theatre

There was talk of a National Theatre from the mid-nineteenth century onwards – Charles Dickens and the poet Matthew Arnold were supporters of the idea – but nothing really happened until the National Theatre Bill was passed in Parliament in 1949, after the war had interrupted a fresh momentum in the campaign. George Bernard Shaw said in 1938, on receipt of the deeds to a site then being excavated opposite the Victoria & Albert Museum in South Kensington, that 'The English people do not want a National Theatre any more than they ever wanted a British Museum or a National Gallery.' His point being that, once built, it would be naturally accepted as an indispensable phenomenon.

And so it has proved. Architect Denys Lasdun's concrete Xanadu (his first, and his only, theatre) rose at last on the South Bank in 1976, greeted by all manner of disapproving commentary – 'Kafka's Castle has been made real' cried the historian A.J.P. Taylor; 'Colditz on Thames' sneered the playwright John Osborne – but receiving an increasingly warm welcome over the years from the general public. People enjoy being in the place, not only in the imperfectly designed theatre auditoria but also in the foyers – the foyers were his 'fourth' auditorium, Lasdun claimed – the cafés, the bookshop, bars and terraces. And after the recent £83 million rebuild and refurbishment, unveiled in 2015, the place opened out to the river, with views and access to outdoor areas that are all part of the South Bank regeneration now stretching eastward to the Tate Modern and Shakespeare's Globe and westward towards the Festival Hall, the London Eye and the Jubilee Gardens.

One thing that sped up the process was, ironically, the

*The Lyttelton Theatre, the National's second auditorium, showing the set design, by Mark Thompson, for* Three Days in the Country. *The concrete exterior is continued inside, with seating for 900.*

*The Lyttelton Theatre front-of-house. Denys Lasdun regarded the National's foyer as its 'fourth auditorium'.*

inauguration of the Royal Shakespeare Company in 1960, which corralled the existing Shakespeare Memorial Theatre in Stratford-upon-Avon and the Aldwych Theatre in London. And Peter Hall, who founded the RSC, much to the annoyance of the NT lobby, was eventually appointed the National's artistic director in 1973 – in succession to Laurence Olivier, who had been the first NT director in Chichester and at the Old Vic from 1962 – and supervised the move across the Thames to the South Bank. It remains a moot point whether the ailing Olivier, who was much hurt at being replaced by the man whom he came to regard as his nemesis, could have managed the strain of opening the new building and running three auditoria and a huge staff. Cometh the hour, cometh the man, and Hall was undoubtedly the right appointment, though his enemies always accused him of vanity and empire-building. Hall battled through triumphantly, but it took him several years – there were endless teething problems, industrial action and unfinished building work – before he settled in and

eventually handed over to Richard Eyre. Not until late 2016, during a celebratory fortieth anniversary conference of technicians, stage-management and administrators, did the much-vaunted Olivier drum revolve – first used in a 1982 production – finally work to its maximum potential at the push of a button.

The whole building was never properly ready to open, and only did so, piece-meal, one theatre at a time. First, in March 1976, the 900-seat, proscenium-arched Lyttelton – so named for Oliver Lyttelton, Lord Chandos, a businessman, MP and first chairman of the National – opened with a clutch of performances including Peggy Ashcroft in Beckett's *Happy Days*, Albert Finney as Hamlet and Ralph Richardson in Ibsen's *John Gabriel Borkman*. Then, in early October of the same year, in the 1,100-seat Olivier, modelled on the Greek open-air amphitheatre at Epidaurus, Finney led a magnificent production of Christopher Marlowe's *Tamburlaine the Great*. The Queen officially opened the building on 25 October before enduring a disastrous Olivier staging of Goldoni's *Il campiello*. Olivier himself spoke only once from the stage that bears his name, and did so on that opening night, finding the 'sweet spot' centre stage, half-way to the front.

The 400-seat courtyard Cottesloe, painted a depressing black at Peter Hall's insistence, was, in the original plans, an orchestral rehearsal room for the new Sadler's Wells opera house that never happened. It rapidly became the company's own favourite auditorium, opening in March 1977 with an eight-hour sci-fi epic *Illuminatus!*, in which – great joke – the recorded voice of a computer was that of John Gielgud, the greatest speaking voice of twentieth-century theatre (the cast included Bill Nighy and Jim Broadbent, both of considerable future fame). There were efforts in the 1980s to have a National Theatre 'company', or several, but only the Bill Bryden company – who did the magical *Mysteries*, later seen in the Lyceum to such good effect – in the Cottesloe ever remotely fitted the bill, and the

NT on the South Bank has become a succession of mostly ad hoc companies for different productions as opposed to the taut, star-laden identity of Olivier's company and operation at the Old Vic.

The place, in truth, is a monumental factory. Between 60 and 80 per cent of everything you see on the stage is made in-house. Every show is scheduled eighteen months in advance and the production is prepared, designed and built twenty weeks in advance of opening. One thousand people work in the building, 100 of them in the workshops. In forty years on the South Bank, nearly 900 shows have been produced. After Olivier, Hall and the board initiated a run of white male artistic directors who, like him, were graduates of Cambridge University: Richard Eyre (in 1988), Trevor Nunn (who had succeeded Hall as artistic director of the RSC, in 1997), and Nicholas Hytner (in 2003). When Rufus Norris succeeded Hytner in 2015, he was the first artistic director, possibly anywhere, to have worked as a

*The dye room.*

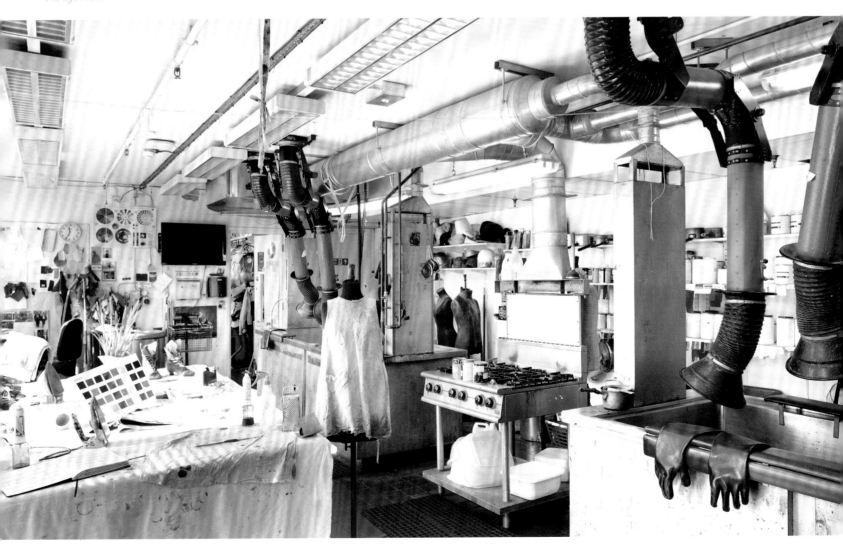

painter and decorator, pop musician and magazine cover model.

Each director has built on the success of his predecessor. There were endless attempts to improve the Olivier's acoustics with panels and microphones, but concrete is an unyielding element; sound does not bounce around and break up in sonic waves as it does when hitting West End balconies and plasterwork. Designers grappled endlessly and heroically with the challenge of the Lyttelton. But remarkable work was achieved nonetheless for the simple reason that putting on a show in any theatre is, to some extent, about overcoming the odds and the difficulties. Eyre tried to narrow the Olivier, but couldn't. Nunn put bleachers into the Lyttelton and then created an informal 'loft' theatre space in the Olivier's front-of-house areas for new plays. Hytner closed the Cottesloe for a year for remodelling and erected a red shed in front of the main entrance and called it the Temporary Theatre; it stayed for three years and proved as popular as any of the 'proper' theatres, and a shot of adrenaline in the arm of the programming. 'A wise architect', said Peter Brook, 'recognises that a theatre must evolve – like an airport.' Lasdun proved impervious to the pleas on all sides to make his theatre seem less like an airport, but gradually, over the years, a combination of familiarity and clever tweaking has done his evolving for him – except inside the Olivier and Lyttelton, which remain sacrosanct in his brutalist, concretised vision and continue to pose every actor, director and designer headaches, however much the audience refuses to complain.

The odd strip of coloured neon lighting 'humanises' the foyers. The bookshop, which had daylight in it, has been moved, more spaciously, but with no daylight, into the body of the main entrance. The box office has jumped to the other side of the main foyer and the long Lyttelton bar is now smaller, and nearer the front of the building on one side. Long benches and tables are provided for tourists, students and informal meetings, as well as for theatre-goers. And much of this happened during the NT Future rebuild masterminded by Hytner and his chief executive Nick Starr, and seen through by Norris and Starr's successor, Lisa

Burger. The Cottesloe is now the Dorfman – Lloyd Dorfman, the philanthropist and founder of Travelex, the company which funds a cheap ticket scheme, donated a cool £10 million to the rebuild – and is pretty much as it was, with improved flexibility, a new flat floor and some higher seating in the galleries. But that old Cottesloe side of the NT is now more open to the river, and there's a new bar on the corner called the Understudy where, presumably, the understudies can spend their evenings hoping not to be called to the stage.

Otherwise, the main new features are two large educational studios, one of them the same rectangular shape as the still operational NT studio next to the Old Vic (where the most successful NT production of all time, *War Horse*, was researched and workshopped) and huge new scene-painting and set-building docks. These are spectacular, as you can see on the guided tours that take you backstage, over walkways, through carpentry benches, property stores and past five rehearsal rooms and the four floors of thirteen dressing rooms (numbered 0 to 12 for superstitious reasons), each with its own window and bed, each looking over an inner courtyard. On first nights, there's a 'banging out' ceremony when all the actors in the other shows lean out of their windows wishing bon voyage to their colleagues about to walk the plank. This is a throwback to 'Richardson's rocket' when the eccentric, mysterious actor, friend and colleague of Olivier at the Old Vic before and after the Second World War – and in the West End in a famous season at the New Theatre (later renamed the Albery, now the Noël Coward) – lit a firework on the roof of the building in March 1976, and on many nights subsequently. Fifty years after it was founded at the Old Vic, and after forty tumultuous years on the South Bank, we now cannot imagine a life, or indeed a theatrical culture, without the National Theatre.

Royal National Theatre

Upper Ground, South Bank, London SE1 9PX

www.nationaltheatre.org.uk

# Royal Court Theatre

The idea that in 2016 we should have been celebrating the sixtieth anniversary of the English Stage Company at the Royal Court must have seemed unthinkable when John Osborne's *Look Back in Anger* opened in the same year as the Suez crisis and gave voice to a new generation of the disaffected young on the British stage for the first time. The play received mixed reviews and played initially to poor houses. But a television extract changed all that and Kenneth Tynan's famous review – 'I doubt if I could love anyone who did not wish to see *Look Back in Anger*. It is the best young play of its decade.' – was later seen to herald a seismic upheaval in the temper and social parameters of the modern British stage.

Still, sixty years is a long time, and the ESC at the Royal Court remains, just about, the most important new writing theatre in Britain, even if good new plays abounding at smaller venues and the National Theatre might just as easily have been presented here. While the Court's reputation has remained a going concern throughout this period, this longevity is undoubtedly due in major part to the theatre itself, a Victorian jewel by Walter Emden (and, to start with, Bertie Crewe) which opened on the east side of Sloane Square in 1888, next door to the entrance to the Metropolitan railway (now Sloane Square Tube) and was reconstructed and re-imagined, while magically remaining itself, by architects Haworth Tompkins in 2000 after a three-year closure.

The first Royal Court, known in 1870 as the New Chelsea, and then the Belgravia Theatre, was a converted chapel on the south side of the square, a site recently occupied by WH Smith newsagents and now a Hugo Boss fashion emporium. The 'new work' tone was undoubtedly set by the plays on that stage by

*The spiritual home of new theatre writing from Bernard Shaw to Caryl Churchill is a miraculously revamped Victorian jewel.*

*The grid, serving technical revolutions in design and lighting since 1956.*

W.S. Gilbert and Arthur Wing Pinero, whose *Trelawny of the Wells*, one of the most delightful English plays about the changing theatre ever written, was then given in the new theatre of change in 1898. The red brick and stone façade of Emden's theatre is still essentially the same, built on four storeys, with a pleasing central pediment proclaiming the theatre's name carved in relief on a stone scroll, applied Corinthian columns and elaborately carved supporting pediments representing the Arts and the Drama on the third-floor outer bays. The main entrance has been altered, but the unassuming four wide stone steps, bookended by stone blocks, have always made the theatre seem both welcoming and special. Since the first days of the ESC, actors and theatre staff have lolled and mingled with passers-by and ticket-buyers, creating a relaxed bohemian atmosphere that slightly worried John Gielgud when he turned up to appear in a David Storey play in 1970; he was expecting to find everyone wearing sandals and reading Proust.

The early Court years were marked by a series of Pinero plays, but the most significant short period is 1904–7 when, under the visionary management of J.E. Vedrenne and Harley Granville-Barker, who had convinced the owners they should present special matinées of Bernard Shaw's *Candida*, there was a rolling repertoire, given in matinées and short runs, of thirty-two plays by seventeen authors, some of them contemporary European (Maeterlinck, Hauptmann, W.B. Yeats), some ancient Greek and many new British, including John Galsworthy and Shaw. No less than eleven sure-fire Shaw plays were seen in this period, including *Man and Superman*, *Major Barbara* and *The Doctor's Dilemma*; here was a pocket version of an ideal 'national theatre' – an ideal Granville-Barker and Shaw both advocated years before it happened. But here, too, was an example for the future Royal Court as founded in the ESC.

The Abbey Theatre of Dublin were regular visitors before the First World War and Shaw returned with *Heartbreak*

*House* in 1921 and the five parts of *Back to Methusela*, performed over four nights in 1922. The theatre sustained its reputation through a rocky period before closing in 1932 for twenty years, with brief bursts as a cinema and a wartime Blitz target. On re-opening under the aegis of property developer Alfred Esdaile – who remained the theatre's licensee right through to the arrival of the ESC – there were revues and, prophetically, the first London production of Brecht and Kurt Weill's *The Threepenny Opera* in February 1956. As this transferred to the Aldwych, George Devine arrived as founding artistic director of the ESC. So began the second great Court era, with classics, as in 1904, serving as box office ballast to the remarkable, though at first less commercially successful, tide of new plays of Osborne, Arnold Wesker, David Storey, John Arden and Edward Bond. Devine was succeeded in 1965 by his protégé William Gaskill, who built bridges with the emergent fringe and brought in such key contemporary writers as David Hare, Christopher Hampton, Ann Jellicoe, Howard Barker, Caryl Churchill, Heathcote Williams and Howard Brenton.

The auditorium was redecorated by the designer Jocelyn Herbert in 1964, there were developed various house styles of Brechtian austerity, white light – the Court was the first London theatre to have a fully visible lighting rig on its stage during a performance – detailed, realistic acting and, because of critical brickbats and squabbles with the Lord Chamberlain (before censorship was abolished, largely thanks to the Court, in 1968) and the Arts Council, an entrenched spirit of defiance that inflamed the work in a way you rarely see now. Gaskill's successors increasingly felt that the building, which was starting to fall down, was simply not fit for purpose, hence the major rebuild and refit which ended up costing £28.5 million including a £3 million gift from the Jerwood Foundation for which they controversially traded their name; the two theatres – the Theatre Upstairs, a studio venue formerly a club and restaurant and originally Granville-Barker's rehearsal room, had opened in 1971 – were now to be labelled the Jerwood Theatre Downstairs and the Jerwood Theatre Upstairs. The former was fitted out with comfortable brown leather seats with airline-style stringy pouches for your programmes or personal effects on the back of the seat in front. The latter was opened right up to the wooden-beamed roof, adding height and airiness to the fabled adaptability of the space.

The rebuild was a difficult and finally extraordinary operation on a cramped site. Steve Tompkins of Haworth Tompkins was prepared to be both radical and reverent, creating a raw, stripped-back environment with some daring excavation work while mindful of the building's history and significance. He always cited the work of the Italian architect Carlo Scarpa as an inspiration, and he studied in particular Scarpa's sensitive and imaginative restoration of the medieval Castelvecchio Museum in Verona before starting work in Sloane Square. While the Royal Court under Stephen Daldry decamped to venues in the West End (the drastically reconfigured Ambassadors and the dismally repainted Duke of York's) the Court was transformed: builders dug down under the theatre and under the road to the square where Daldry and the architects hoped that a disused ladies' lavatory would link the square to the new subterranean theatre restaurant and bar. The Cadogan Estate, which owns this area of London, and the local Royal Borough of Kensington and Chelsea, refused permission for this imaginative suggestion, though the stairs up to the square from the back of the restaurant can still be used in a fire or evacuation emergency.

In the theatre itself, the walls were stripped back to the brick, a great cylindrical red drum rising through the theatre behind the back of the seating, the two horseshoe circles clad behind in riveted, burning metal plating, like the hull of a ship. Somehow, there appeared unimaginable well-appointed offices and lavatories in a new wing to the side of the theatre in the alley, where once the accounts department was housed in a makeshift Portakabin. There's a new lift to take you from foyer level to the Jerwood Theatre Upstairs, though the slow trudge upwards is worth it for the ingeniously inserted mini-banquettes on the way and the historic poster display on the evocative brick walls. Snowdon's great photograph of George Devine is on the other side of the building, en route to the dress circle bar, which gives, in its intimate loggia, onto the square and its non-stop hubbub of buses and tourists preparing to advance along the King's Road, still one of London's great thoroughfares, now modified with the Saatchi Gallery of contemporary art (which opened in 1985) and inviting new public spaces just beyond the Peter Jones department store.

When Laurence Olivier played the decrepit vaudevillian Archie Rice in Osborne's *The Entertainer* at the Royal Court in 1957, he joshed the audience with, 'Don't clap too hard . . . it's a very old building.' Well it is, but it's been reborn. On first seeing the new Court in 2000, the architectural critic Jonathan Glancey hailed 'a dreamlike world, an architectural magic lantern show, a grease-paint realm of shadows and half-light' and likened the passageways and ironwork to 'the feel of Captain Nemo's *Nautilus*' in Jules Verne's *Twenty Thousand Leagues Under the Sea*. The Royal Court sails on through calm and storm, but is usually seen at its best in choppy waters. They seem to have absorbed the advice of a character in Tennessee Williams' *Camino Real*, echoing the example of both Harley Granville-Barker and George Devine: 'Make voyages . . . attempt them . . . there is nothing else!'

Royal Court Theatre

Sloane Square, London SW1W 8AS

www.royalcourttheatre.com

*The dress circle has the same comfortable leather seating as the rest of the auditorium, as does the upper circle, whose riveted metal cladding lends an industrial touch.*

# Roundhouse

The Roundhouse, known as the Round House prior to a spectacular £30 million redevelopment twenty years ago, has had as many lives as the proverbial cat: engine shed, gin warehouse, left-wing arts centre, rock venue, avant-garde theatre, outpost of the Proms (the BBC's annual classical musical festival), dance house and educational facility, some of these functions rolling promiscuously into each other. But there are two clear historical phases: mid-nineteenth century to closure in 1983, and a new dawn in 1996 thanks to the intervention of entrepreneur Torquil Norman, founder of Bluebird Toys, who purchased the place from Camden Council for £6.5 million as part of his children and young people's charity. The common feature to both eras, apart from the iconic circular architecture, is the idea of social and scientific facility, from the new steam engines to the underground warren of workshops, recording studios and computer stations. Commuters and students who've slipped through the net of the travel and educational systems are often the worst catered for by the authorities; the Roundhouse has done its bit by each group.

The place was built by George Stephenson, father of British locomotives and the railway, in London brick in 1846 and intended as a terminus for trains from the new East Midlands line. But, after protests akin to our own public brouhaha over a third runway at Heathrow, a Bill of Parliament decreed the engines should be uncoupled at Chalk Farm and the carriages shunted noiselessly into Euston. The roof of wooden beams gathered to a dome-like cupola, the interior diameter marked by a circle of twenty-four elegant iron pillars which created bays and repair pits with a capacity for twenty-three engines arriving onto a central turntable. When the engines became too big to be accommodated, the Roundhouse became a goods shed and

*The circular Roundhouse retains the two dozen slender arches that accommodated steam engines for repair.*

in 1869 was leased to W. & A. Gilbey, purveyors of Gilbey's Gin – so that was the interval drinks sorted well in advance of any performance in the place – but gradually declined in usage and repair until in 1967 the Round House Trust secured the freehold from British Rail. The trust had been formed partly to support the application for occupancy by Centre 42, a cultural initiative aimed at the participation of the working class by the playwright Arnold Wesker, supported by the Trades Unions; item 42 on the agenda of the TUC conference in 1960 had been an enquiry into the state of the arts. At this point, staircases were built, repairs carried out, lighting installed and, after the Labour Party election victory of 1964, Prime Minister Harold Wilson was recruited as a supporter, too. Wilson recommended George Hoskins, an economist and businessman, as fundraiser and adviser. While Wesker arranged 'people's festivals' around Britain, Hoskins rolled up his sleeves and launched the theatre in 1968 with an experimental version of *The Tempest* directed by Peter Brook, with rock concerts as a commercial venture to support Centre 42.

This mixture of striking new theatre and rock defined the Roundhouse: Brook was followed by the Living Theatre of New York, who stripped off and invited the audience to join in an orgy, and Steven Berkoff in Kafka's *Metamorphosis*. The Doors and Jim Morrison made their only appearance in Britain here, and Jimi Hendrix and the Rolling Stones gave concerts. When, in 1970, Wesker formed a company to perform his own play, *The Friends*, the box office was a disaster. Hoskins promptly booked Kenneth Tynan's nude revue *Oh! Calcutta!* (the title was taken from a French surreal painting of a reclining nude: 'Oh, quel cul t'as!') and Wesker resigned in a fury. A poster display on the circle level documents another form of outrage, one typical after the abolition of censorship in 1968. A bespectacled Greater London Council member for Bromley, Frank Smith, wrote, in the wake of *Oh! Calcutta!* that the show 'was complete sex from start to finish' and that his wife, Ida, 'had been upset ever since'.

Thereafter the Roundhouse presented Nicol Williamson's coruscating *Hamlet*, for which the programme printed a

*The roof of wooden beams gathers to a dome-like cupola.*

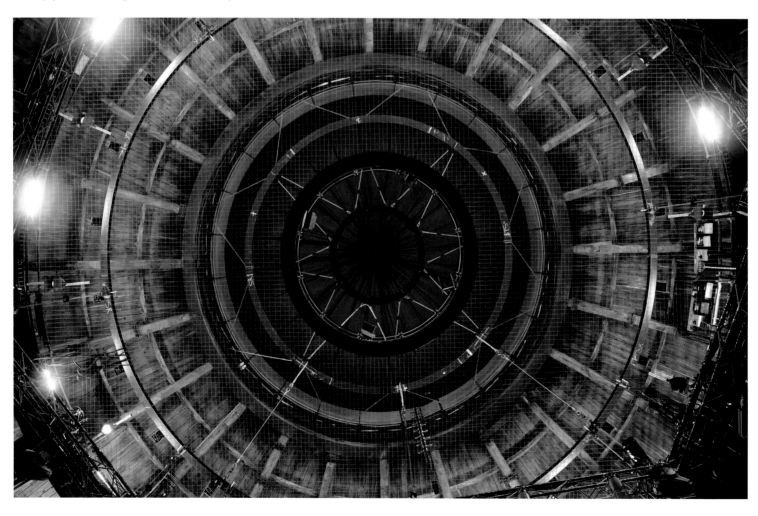

*The venue has hosted rock concerts, design exhibitions and many wild parties.*

manifesto: 'Now a new revolution is needed to destroy, finally and completely, the form of the proscenium theatre and the social habits that go with it.' In that spirit, fuelled by the adaptability and circus-like propensities of the arena, international avant-garde companies made a beeline for north London and created a succession of outrageous spectacles, including a fairground staging of the French Revolution as a sideshow on carts trundling between the columns. Hoskins and his successor, Thelma Holt, invited companies from abroad and in the regions to explore the special atmosphere of this elegant shed and its dimly lit long bar that was something of a local hippie destination.

After the 1983 closure, performances were sporadic and new plans uninspired. Money was raised and spent on a new roof designed by Richard Rodgers. Then, in 1996, when Torquil Norman put his cards on the table, a new trust was formed to raise funds for the rebuild and restoration. In a new climate of arts sponsorship, funding partners fell over themselves to join in; they were the Arts Council, the Heritage Lottery Fund, the London Development Agency, the Department for Education and Skills, and the Foundation for Sport and the Arts. Everyone, it seemed, was fired up by an affection for the Roundhouse as a building and as a renewed cultural hub and agency. The roof was sand-blasted and sound-proofed to a hundred decibels. The ash pits where the engines were repaired were dug out, the tunnels restored, the underground vaults and passages re-rendered. Over the past ten years, apart from the influx of broadcasting, music-making, digital mixing and circus skills courses in

the underground labyrinth, involving local schools and 'difficult' students from the Pupil Referral Unit, there have been 4,000 performances and ticket sales of £3 million. The listings magazine *Time Out* is, it declares on the doors of the ground floor rest rooms in bright red glazed brick, 'flushed with pride to sponsor these toilets'. An adhesive strip across the front doors carries the repeated legend, 'Creativity drives Change drives Creativity drives Change drives . . .'

Aside from the rock concerts, which are as popular as ever, the performance side of things has drifted more into circus, poetry, and spoken sound rather than theatre. But one of the endearing characteristics of the gloriously informal Roundhouse is that you never really know what is going to happen next. They are as likely to send in the clowns as swing from the roof on trapezes. On the Primrose Hill side of the building there is now a long curved new section, attached like an extra limb on its circular body; this is where the old car park used to be, and it now houses offices and, in summer months, a terrace bar and even a beach . . . which takes us right back to the mid-1970s, when mime artist Lindsay Kemp, David Bowie's mentor, performed in a sort of seaside diversion, *Mr Punch's Pantomime*, a glorious hotch-potch of Victorian couplets, commedia dell'arte and high camp; the show would still seem quintessentially 'Roundhouse' if revived tomorrow.

Roundhouse
Chalk Farm Road, London NW1 8EH
www.roundhouse.org.uk

# Regent's Park Open Air Theatre

Open air theatre in parks and gardens is a defining characteristic of the English summer, however chill, wet and gloomy. We love to sit and suffer in silence, making a virtue of itchy rugs and mulled wine, holding in our minds the ideal circumstances of an enchanting production of *A Midsummer Night's Dream* performed between dusk and dark at the end of a still, hot summer afternoon, with the birds quietening, the tall trees swaying in the gentlest breeze and the glimmer of artificial light invading the natural beauty of glade, copse and bosky arbour. That is the image we have of the grandest of all our open air theatres: in Regent's Park, situated between the formal Italian gardens and Queen Mary's rose garden on the park's Inner Circle, lined with poplar, sycamore and hazel – the most glorious, silent and long-standing extras in the business – and approached across lawns scattered with deck chairs, trees and hedges, close by a magnificent Triton fountain in which a muscular merman blows on his conch while naked bronze ladies revel in the spume at his fin, a tableau that seems to proclaim a night of theatrical adventure.

The first Shakespeare on the site of the current theatre was provided by the so-called Woodland Players, directed by Ben Greet, in 1900, when Regent's Park was known as the Royal Botanical Gardens. In 1932, the producer Sydney Carroll was allowed to present four matinées of a 'black and white' *Twelfth Night* imported from the West End. A year later, Carroll was granted a licence, and the theatre opened on 5 June 1933 with the same *Twelfth Night*, directed by the colourful actor-manager Robert ('Look here, old son . . .') Atkins, watched by an audience upwards of 3,000. Carroll, who was prone to making long speeches at the curtain calls, was particularly proud of the new turf laid by a firm in Surrey for the second season in 1934. With

*A set design, by Max Jones, for Jane Austen's* Pride and Prejudice *proved that the natural home for outdoor Shakespeare could adapt to embrace Regency classicism.*

*The 1975 stage and auditorium were refitted in the 2012 update. The Park became a new modern theatre without a roof.*

the massed ranks of the cast standing patiently behind him, he declared, 'Ladies and Gentlemen, I want you to know that every sod on this stage comes from Richmond.'

Shakespeare was always the main attraction, but the theatre had a long association, too, with George Bernard Shaw, who wrote *The Six of Calais* specifically for the park in that second season, after taking issue both with Rodin (whose sculpture had much moved him) and with Froissart's chronicles on the niceties of King Edward III's demands of the six burghers at the long-running siege. In those early years, the audience sat on ground-level deckchairs and slatted park benches to the rear. Shrubs were planted to define a newly built stage in front of the existing trees and the prompter crouched beneath a privet hedge. Lights and speakers were hung around in the trees. Announcements from the stage were made by an elderly Ben Greet, who had been invited back with the honorary title of Master of the Greensward.

Robert Atkins directed all the productions and succeeded Carroll as overall director in 1939. Atkins conducted his

auditions in The Volunteer pub at the top of Baker Street, where the resident parrot was not discouraged from squawking at, and then attacking, the suppliant actors. Star names on the pre-war cast lists included Gladys Cooper, Vivien Leigh, Anna Neagle, Balliol Holloway, Leslie French, Griffith Jones and Jack Hawkins. The facilities and the scenery were rudimentary and, when the rain came, the performance continued in an uncomfortable marquee. Atkins, whose roles included Toby Belch, Bottom and Caliban, remained undaunted during the war and, save for a short 'sabbatical' of two seasons in charge of the Memorial Theatre at Stratford-upon-Avon, struggled on through the 1950s, with mounting financial crises, a complete shutdown in 1954, declining standards, appalling weather in 1960 and another closure in 1961. Atkins, whose career had begun in the sunset of the Edwardian actor-managers, at last conceded defeat, and retired.

The Department of the Environment invited tenders for the Park's future in *The Stage* newspaper and the actor David Conville, abetted by the director David William, both in their thirties and already vastly experienced, applied successfully for what looked like a lost cause at worst and a great challenge at best. They found a scene of dilapidation, no fixed seating or lighting, no office, no records, no tent. With Peter Hall in charge of the fledgling Royal Shakespeare Company and Laurence Olivier launching the National Theatre, Conville rolled up his sleeves, raised money, signed up actors, fixed the lighting and brought in Clement Freud to do the catering. He created the New Shakespeare Company, opening in 1962 with, of course, the *Dream* (Patrick Wymark as Bottom, David William as Oberon and Heather Chasen – 'like a piece of animated Dresden china' said one critic – as Helena).

The stage was reconstructed but remained impossibly wide, and the audience of about 1,500 was still seated in deckchairs. But momentum was gathering. Conville led the company on British Council tours abroad, the Arts Council offered more help and sponsorship grew through donations and charity galas. The result, opening in the late summer of 1975, at a cost of £150,000, was a new amphitheatre of 1,200 steeply raked tip-up seats. Toilets and dressing rooms were further enhanced and improved. 'Is there any air-conditioning?' asked an American visitor. Conville, stationed near the box office, kept a straight face and said 'Yes.'

The longest bar in the London theatre shaped up beneath the raised second tier in the auditorium, and hamburgers and sausages sizzled at the far end. The programme each year was mostly Shakespearean comedies, though in 1976 Robert Stephens played Othello – probably the last white actor to 'black up' in the role – with Edward Fox as Iago. The Arts Council started to blow more cold than hot about the Park and cut the modest grant of £25,000 completely in 1981. The producer Peter Saunders promptly wrote Conville a cheque for that amount and saved the theatre from closure. The fiftieth anniversary was marked with a royal visit by the Queen and Prince Philip on 12 July 1982 to see Shaw's *Dark Lady of the Sonnets*, in which the character of Shakespeare breaks into Whitehall Palace 'almost to the very door of the Queen's chamber'; three days earlier, in a notable breach of security, a man had shinned up a drainpipe at Buckingham Palace and entered the Queen's bedroom, claiming later to have sat on the bed chatting to Her Majesty before she raised the alarm.

Ian Talbot, who had first played here in 1971 – he, like Atkins, was a renowned and regular Bottom – was installed as Conville's successor in 1987, and established an annual repertoire of two major Shakespeares and a musical,

widening the traditional pastoral brief into the tragedies and romances. Ralph Fiennes and Hugh Bonneville made their professional debuts in the Park, and Damian Lewis played Hamlet in 1994. Major improvements were made in 1999: a Robert Atkins studio was opened for small-scale performances and hospitality, the picnic lawn was enlarged, the bar modified and redesigned, and the seats remodelled in two banks of nine rows in the lower tier, ten in the upper. Two major entrances were established under the top rake.

The theatre remains an entirely self-funded charity and, when Timothy Sheader was appointed artistic director in succession to Talbot in 2007, he and his joint chief executive, William Village, initiated a more general programming policy, partly in response to the ongoing success of Shakespeare's Globe but also to try and establish the Park as a mainstream producing theatre in London beyond its Shakespearean remit. So the past ten years have seen revivals of Arthur Miller's *The Crucible*, Nigel Williams' *Lord of the Flies*, Chekhov and Oscar Wilde, James Lapine and Stephen Sondheim's *Into the Woods* and *The Sound of Music* as well as usually just one Shakespeare a season, sometimes none at all.

In 2012, seating was replaced, the bar once again redesigned, wooden offices constructed behind the stage – for many years the offices were off-site – with new workshops, wardrobe and dressing rooms. The stage was flattened at the front and a concrete base laid down to allow for much more scenic diversity and there are plans afoot for a further £3.5 million development of on-site rehearsal rooms and an improved kitchen and staff facilities. There is a new dining area overlooking the long bar, with waiter service, and the Robert Atkins Studio is now used solely for corporate and individual sponsors' hospitality and functions.

Some things never change. The aeroplanes always fly over at moments of deepest silence in the auditorium, and Feste's intoning of 'The rain it raineth every day' always goes down well. Even in the rainiest seasons, though, very few performances are lost. There is no marquee – Conville did away with that early on – so customers can reschedule another performance if theirs is interrupted or abandoned. And the magic is still palpable, even if we no longer have those trademark, tantalising glimpses of Palladian mansions, balustraded stairways and Ionic columns among the greenery; a modern, more brutalist design ethic has invaded the arena and challenged the Arcadian idyll.

Regent's Park Open Air Theatre

Inner Circle, Regents Park, London NW1 4NU

www.openairtheatre.com

INFORMAL DELIGHTS

50

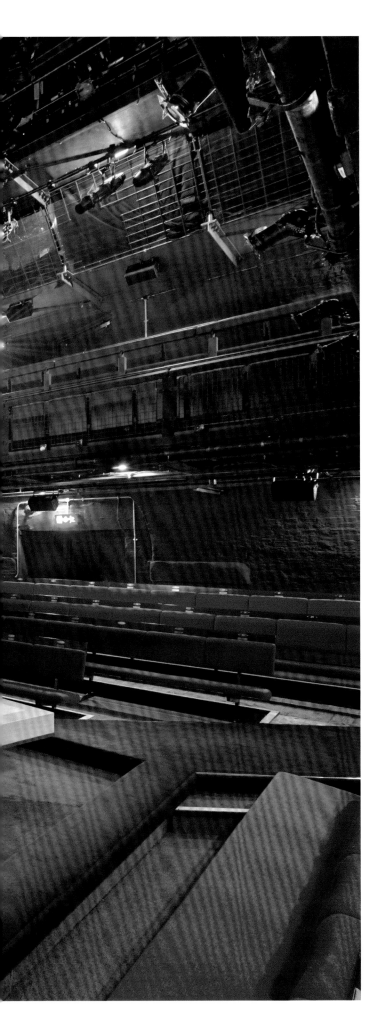

# Donmar Warehouse

There's a confusion abroad over the name of this 252-seat 'not-for-profit' attic West End powerhouse, one of the most important creative venues in London, in the heart of Covent Garden. It has been suggested that 'Donmar' is an amalgam of 'Don' as in Donald Albery, the great impresario who owned the place as a storehouse and rehearsal room in the 1960s – and whose son, Ian Albery, was a producing administrator there with Nica Burns in the 1980s – and 'Mar' as in Margot Fonteyn, the prima ballerina who was a very close, and long-standing, friend of the 'Don'. In fact, the 'Mar' part belongs to the second name of Albery's second wife, Cecily Margaret H. Boys, and even if it didn't, the more likely 'Mar' could have been claimed by Dame Alicia Markova, who founded the London Festival Ballet in 1950, with Anton Dolin, and who rehearsed in the Donmar with that company (which became the English National Ballet in 1989) during the late 1960s when Albery was their producer and administrator. Margot Fonteyn had no direct connection with the ENB, dancing with the Royal Ballet, and other premier companies, all her professional life.

Today, the Donmar is a three-sided grey-painted auditorium with a gallery, and a superb theatrical height and unexpected spaciousness – a large cube, in fact, measuring 25 feet in all directions – that retains the feel of its late-nineteenth-century origins as a brewery vat room and hop storage, with stabling underneath. There were further associations with both a film studio and a banana-ripening storage depot for the adjacent market that led to Ian Albery acquiring a lease in 1960 as an important rehearsal studio for, among other shows, his own father's production of Lionel Bart's *Oliver!*. Donald Albery,

OPPOSITE *The lighting rig at the top of a space that is an almost perfect cube, measuring 25 feet in all directions.*

son of the legendary Sir Bronson, was managing director of the Albery (now the Noël Coward), Criterion, Piccadilly, Wyndham's, as well as the Donmar, and sold them all on when he retired in 1977. The Donmar was instantly assigned to the Royal Shakespeare Company, who launched a lively and often remarkable programme of new plays, including *Educating Rita* by Willy Russell, over the next five years. The Warehouse, as it was now more generally known, became the 'new work' conscience of the RSC under the leadership of younger directors such as Howard Davies and Bill Alexander.

The theatre, then as now, was at the top of a staircase, the frontage on Earlham Street always unprepossessing, the interior unfussy and straightforward as befits a building externally constructed in London stock brick with metal-framed windows. When the RSC moved out to take up their allotted residency in the Barbican in 1981 (where the Warehouse repertoire was consigned to the bunker-like Pit two floors below ground level), Ian Albery and Nica Burns ran the venue as a producing theatre, launching the cabaret trio Fascinating Aida and creating a welcome home for leading small-scale touring companies, notably Cheek by Jowl run by the director Declan Donnellan and designer Nick Ormerod.

The last twenty-five years have seen this reputation developed and enhanced under the successive artistic directorships of Sam Mendes, Michael Grandage and Josie Rourke, ownership moving through Ambassador Theatre Group (ATG) to the Donmar itself, who purchased the site on a 125-year lease effective from early 2017, with ATG maintaining a management contract. The theatre was reconstructed and expanded as part of the commercial development in the adjoining Neal's Yard at the start of Sam Mendes' tenancy, with new bars and toilets on both levels. The auditorium has bench seating on three sides at two levels, although the benches downstairs have lately been marked off as individual seats. The muted colour scheme varies, but grey is usually the order of the day on carpets and walls, with distinctive 'warehouse' wooden floors in the two main gangways and surrounds.

Like the Almeida, the Donmar has its own version of epic intimacy, the new style favoured even in the larger arenas of the RSC and National, where rhetorical acting and 'big beast' turns of any kind are rare. So, the Donmar has been as adept at presenting domestic drama and close-up musicals with sleek interpolated design as it has been in reviving German classics or Shakespeare, especially so when fully exploiting the scenic potential of the brick back wall, usually painted black. The Donmar has compiled an impressive back catalogue of West End and Broadway transfers, creating a sense of this small, highly sponsored, élitist space – though it does sell £10 tickets on the day and allows twenty people to stand at the back of the gallery – radiating outwards. Derek Jacobi, for instance, played King Lear for a hefty run in Covent Garden before touring nationally and broadcasting live in cinemas around the world under the aegis of the National Live scheme; that one performance in February 2011 was seen by over 30,000 people on 350 screens in twenty countries. Michael Grandage presented a season of Donmar plays in the West End and Josie Rourke has mounted an all-female Shakespeare trilogy – with Harriet Walter playing Brutus, Henry IV and Prospero – in

a temporary 420-seat theatre at King's Cross station before taking the entire production to Brooklyn.

It's a restrained form of empire-building going on – Sam Mendes and Michael Grandage now run an independent theatre and film production company each and Josie Rourke is increasingly drawn to New York – that wisely stays rooted in the little magic space at the top of the stairs. Meanwhile, another small nineteenth-century warehouse property has been acquired for renovation and occupation – offices, rehearsal rooms, educational and support facilities – five minutes around the corner in Dryden Street. The conversion of this marvellous space, completed in 2013, was by Haworth Tompkins and shared some characteristics with their work on the Royal Court ten years earlier: stripped back and partially demolished walls and ceilings were left in a deliberately 'raw' state, and a new polychromatic staircase,

hand-painted by Anton Malinowski, serves as the warm heart of the building, just as his startling red drum rises like a fiery furnace through the renovated Royal Court. There is even an apartment available for any visiting Broadway star or out-of-town cast member. The ground-level 'green room', running along the outer wall on Dryden Street, with a kitchen, sofas and tables, big windows and a high ceiling, is the social and creative backstage nexus of the whole Donmar operation, where scripts are read, discussed and even written, while actors break for coffee and associates and supporters drop in for meetings and the latest project news.

Donmar Warehouse
41 Earlham Street, London WC2H 9LX
www.donmarwarehouse.com

# The Young Vic

There is nothing fixed, immutable or even hierarchical about the Young Vic. Everyone comes through the same front door – playgoers, drinkers at the bar, actors, deliverymen, schoolchildren – the highly adaptable seating is democratically arranged on oat-coloured benches hugging the acting area, whether that area is a thrust stage or a traverse platform, and 10 per cent of that seating is free to local schools and groups. 'There is', says artistic director David Lan, who has been in the post since 2000, 'nothing like this elsewhere in London or even in New York; it's an image vision of how we'd like to live.'

At the same time, the Young Vic has managed the clever trick of being a real community theatre that is as internationally minded as the Barbican, attracting the best of European directors – Peter Brook, Luc Bondy, Patrice Chéreau, Ivo van Hove – with fruitful creative links to South Africa, Iceland and Australia, as well as with our own leading directors, such as Katie Mitchell, Richard Jones, Sacha Wares and Joe Hill-Gibbins. You don't even have to go to a show to experience the pull and the bounce of the place; most of the people in the 'destination' bar, which has an upper level and an outdoor terrace overlooking The Cut thoroughfare, which runs from the Old Vic along the road to Southwark Tube station, don't buy theatre tickets.

No other London theatre exudes such a mood of improvisation and expectancy. And that is because the Young Vic was never intended, in the first place, to last more than a few years. It was built on a bomb site in 1970 as an outpost of the National Theatre, which was then housed at the Old Vic, under the direction of one of Laurence Olivier's NT associates, Frank Dunlop, with the specific remit of providing a repertoire of new and classic work for younger audiences performed by young NT actors.

*The set design for* A Man of Good Hope *by Isango Ensemble, one of the Young Vic's regular visiting companies in a repertoire as local as it is international.*

The opening show was a riotous version of Molière's *Scapino*, with a sung finale of Italian kitchen gobbledegook that Dunlop and his leading actor, Jim Dale, had composed while studying a menu over dinner in a nearby Italian café. There was an actress in that company, too, called Denise Coffey, who was the nearest our stage has come in the past few decades to a born funny-bones clown. It was a 'good time' theatre that took itself seriously enough to be serious, too.

By 1974, the Young Vic had severed its parental ties to the NT, continuing on its merry, irreverent way through the next fifteen years, slowing down for some imposing Arthur Miller revivals in the 1980s before stalling and running into trouble. It was rescued by a noisy campaign to save the place from the demolition ball in 1990. The next few years under director Tim Supple defined the Young Vic again as a place of magic and mystery for young audiences, with some spectacular reclamation work on the Grimm fairy tales and the Arabian Nights stories. That strand, as well as Dunlop's

track record in knockabout classics and the Pop Theatre he subsequently founded at the Edinburgh Festival, have been fused in a more temperate but always highly imaginative and usually daring house style under Lan.

The artistic roots of the place run deep. The first Young Vic company was founded in 1946 as an offshoot of the short-lived Old Vic Theatre School. Dunlop and the NT were building on that legacy when they hit on the bomb site and architect Bill Howell built his breezeblock and steel-frame building which retains – to this day – the butchers' hooks and green patterned tiles of the original shop. The address – Wilson Brothers, 66 The Cut – is still discernible above the front door. This small stretch was a terrace of shops and houses. Indeed, one house still protrudes, oddly and intriguingly, above the entrance. There was a bakery next door with an air raid shelter in the basement where fifty-four people were killed in a direct hit by the Luftwaffe on 17 April 1941. There is a simple commemorative plaque on an outer wall of the new

OPPOSITE *The wardrobe department.*

OVERLEAF *The stark simplicity of the Young Vic, at once always the same and highly adaptable, a crucible of democratic endeavour.*

rebuild on Greet Street where, incidentally, you can often see directly into the magnificent new workshop, once an open yard with a tin shed in it. And you can also see the carpenters and scenic artists at work, as you do these days on backstage tours of the National and Covent Garden.

The bomb victims are listed by name in a framed scroll inside the theatre, too. This archaeological approach, the process of including the past in the refurbishment of the present, and not just in the raw brickwork, is part of what Steve Tompkins, of Haworth Tompkins, who took on the £12.5 million rebuild in 2004, calls 'the architecture of continuity and accretion'. It reflects exactly the experience of most theatre-goers whose recurring visits to the same building, even an informal one, are limed with an impasto of past performances. The new Young Vic is wrapped around the footprint of the old so that, in the auditorium itself, not all that much has changed, below the first gallery, forty years on; above, it's part of the rebuild, and the roof is very much higher. The auditorium walls used to be dull breezeblock, sometimes black. Now they are painted 'Arab red', giving off a warm red glow not dissimilar to the atmosphere in the Bouffes du Nord in Paris.

On entering the building, you turn left into the main bar area. Look up, and you understand how the structure has been reinforced with a square arrangement of red steel girders beneath a fine, plain wooden roof. Ascending the interior stairs to the second level you pass posters of recent productions set off against the repaired brickwork. The outline of the lintel and pediment on a bricked-in side window in the one remaining house above the entrance is visible. At this level, too, are the new offices, wardrobe, several rehearsal or meeting rooms and the third, tiny

auditorium, the Clare (70 seats), so named for Clare Venables, who died too young at sixty, an inspirational director in London, Lincoln and Sheffield. The second studio theatre, although entered at the first level, has been pushed further back from its initial ground-level footprint and is named the Maria (150 seats) for the great designer Maria Bjornson, who died even younger than Venables. Both these artists died before the rebuild got under way in 2004. Their spirit imbues the house, a very different thing from being a theatre ghost. They represented the best of British 'can-do' in the arts, an indomitable flair and gusto.

David Lan wants all his directors to exploit the opportunities of the building to its limit, and it's therefore not unusual to find yourself sitting in an improvised corrida for a Jacobean tragedy, or filing through unfamiliar corridors en route to Elsinore, or watching a Spanish or modern American classic played out behind glass, enacted in a fresh alignment of the arena's planes and angles as the whole stage revolves imperceptibly towards the next scene or location. Both studios have the same bench seating as in the main house, where the places are numbered. The front-of-house area is considerably extended and the double storey glazing adds light and brightness to the interior. The building, though still modest and unpretentious, is extremely attractive from the street and is clad in a steel mesh that protects the yellow painted surfaces from the sun while suggesting the idea of an industrial factory between shifts when the lights have dimmed and the audience gone home.

The Young Vic

66 The Cut, London SE1 8LZ

www.youngvic.org

# Almeida Theatre

More than any of the newer powerhouses in the London theatre, the Almeida in Islington has extended its projects into other 'found' venues while maintaining a constant process of transformation in its exterior facilities and inner auditorium, which is both intimate – with padded bench seating for 320 – and, because of the height and shape of the building, of potentially epic proportions. Whereas the Victorian and Edwardian theatres of the West End are recovered relics of a golden age of theatrical architecture, the Almeida is a modernised and imaginative response to another kind of early Victorian 1837 establishment, a lecture hall, for the neighbourhood's Scientific and Literary Institution, with a handsomely proportioned, unadorned white frontage of stern columns and tall windows, a step away from the main road, Upper Street, running between Highbury Corner and the Angel.

So there's never been an issue of inherited plasterwork, statuary or stage practice, although it's almost certain that, in those days of medical demonstrations and the 'Elephant Man', there would have been the occasional freak show of conjoined twins or bearded ladies. The seating bank in the 600-seat amphitheatre-like lecture hall was where the theatre's curved back brick wall now encloses the stage action. The upper floor, now the circle area, housed a small natural history museum, committee room and library; the basement, where now there are dressing rooms and the wardrobe, had a small warren of study rooms and caretaker's quarters.

The institute was dissolved in 1872 and its assets sold off. The new owners opened a club for local gentlemen to read newspapers and play billiards, but by 1890 the place was commandeered by the Salvation Army as a new citadel, and

*The Almeida fits snugly and discreetly inside a Victorian lecture hall in Islington, north London.*

*The theatre opened in 1981, this dressing room under the stage dating from a major upgrade in 2003.*

they removed all the smaller rooms and the division of two floors, creating something more like the present arrangement with a large hall facing the curved wall, and a new balcony. The Salvation Army moved out in 1956, selling the premises to a local businessman, Mr Beck, who packed carnival novelties – masks, balloons, party hats – and sold and hired out fancy dress attire and circus equipment; this was the warehouse and despatch centre for his nearby shop on Upper Street. Beck's Carnival Novelties replaced the pews and platforms where the Salvation Army bands played hymns with a small office and piled-high boxes and packing parcels. As the building fell into disrepair in the 1960s, new owners were sought – theatre companies were mooted – but Mr Beck himself, a secret transvestite, was murdered in 1971 in his cottage in Wales by his brother-in-law; the Press cited his links with mobsters and cross-dressers in the criminal underworld, and the business closed down.

It used to be said – though not recently – that Beck's ghost was seen loitering in the theatre absorbing the interval chat about make-up, drag and dressing up. After local residents fought to save the building from demolition, Beck's derelict emporium was bought and 'rediscovered' (paint and plaster chiselled laboriously from the brickwork) by the director Pierre Audi and two university friends, Will Bowen and Chris Naylor, in the mid-1970s. Their inspiration was Peter Brook's Bouffes du Nord in Paris, a similarly derelict 1876 music hall that Brook and his colleagues relaunched – preserving the 'distressed' atmosphere of the place in its brickwork and architectural features – as a Centre of International Theatre Research (and production) in 1974.

The new Almeida Theatre Company was launched at the Edinburgh Festival in 1979 and the building finally opened as the Almeida Theatre in 1981 with a Grade II listing and a series of stark, and startling, productions of classics, visiting companies such as Shared Experience and Complicite, and a contemporary music festival. When Audi moved on into the world of European opera, and handed over to the director/actor partnership of Jonathan Kent and Ian McDiarmid in 1990, this transition heralded a decade of galloping sponsorship, star power, glamour, and stage design, starting, ironically, to obscure the brickwork once again. The company's offices were on Upper Street, further towards the Angel, the other side of The King's Head pub theatre, one of the first London fringe venues.

The Almeida's local empire was extended into other resonant venues. Ralph Fiennes played Hamlet for the Almeida at the Hackney Empire; Hamlet's mother, Gertrude, was Francesca Annis, who became Fiennes' off-stage lover over the next ten years, thus giving a Freudian rewrite to the old adage, formed in answer to the time-honoured academic question, 'Does Hamlet sleep with Ophelia?' 'Yes, dear, but only on tour.' Then, in 2000, Fiennes played both Richard II and Coriolanus for the Almeida colonising the old Gainsborough Studios in Shoreditch, once a railway power station, whisky-bottling plant and warehouse for Oriental rugs, pending redevelopment as apartments; Alfred Hitchcock shot both *The Lodger* and *The Lady Vanishes* there. This was a clever redesign by Haworth Tompkins who, in 2001, wrought another sensitive refurbishment of a found space: a derelict (soon to be demolished) bus depot at King's Cross, while the Almeida itself underwent its drastic reinvention. Again, the King's Cross venue had its industrial interior left raw, and the roof and gable were turfed in sedum; the project was completed in just seventeen weeks. The place opened, with a physically and scenically remarkable production of David Hare's translation of Chekhov's early play *Platonov*, on 11 September 2001.

Kent and McDiarmid were succeeded by Michael Attenborough, who opened the new Almeida in 2003 with Ibsen's *Lady from the Sea* directed by Trevor Nunn, with the late Natasha Richardson (tragically killed in a skiing accident in 2009) in the lead. The £7.6 million refurbishment, funded by the Arts Council and a capital appeal, was most distinguished by the rebuilt foyer, a glass atrium with steel

*The below-stage wardrobe has one of the steel pillars installed by the Salvation Army in 1890 running through.*

and concrete elements, a striking new L-shaped bar and café area; improved seating; and a major backstage upgrade. And when Rupert Goold succeeded Attenborough in 2013, the West End and Broadway transfers intensified and the transformation process now included the cockpit auditorium itself: Simon Stephens' contemporary urban retelling of *Carmen* brought the disc-like stage into the audience, with a bull's carcass greeting them on arrival; Mike Bartlett's *Game* divided the audience, all wearing headphones, into four zones, watching a homeless couple through artificial apertures, like bird-watchers in a hide; and Leo Butler's *Boy* created a violent configuration – almost a work of installation art – featuring supermarket check-outs, West End cut-outs and characters mobilised on travelators, like baggage at an airport. The original shape, if not the brickwork, of the building was honoured when Ralph Fiennes returned in 2016 to play Richard III, the stage dominated by a great hanging steel cylindrical coronet, the circle still supported by the eight slender pillars installed by the Salvation Army over a hundred years previously.

Almeida Theatre
Almeida Street, London N1 1TA
www.almeida.co.uk

*The lighting is pre-set before a performance of* Richard III. *The original lecture hall's seating was on the stage, with a natural history museum in the gallery seating.*

# Tricycle Theatre

The palimpsest of the dynamic little Tricycle Theatre on Kilburn High Road is as densely enriched as any of the big London houses, originating in a medieval King's Cross pub with connections to Robin Hood and settling, suitably enough, in a 1929 Foresters' Hall, which itself had been previously used as a cinema, music and dance hall and temporary offices for the local council of Brent.

And now, another transformation, as the Tricycle undergoes a £5.5 million rebuild, mostly centred on its distinctive auditorium, modelled in 1980 by architect Tim Foster and theatre consultant Iain Mackintosh on the Georgian Theatre Royal in Richmond, Yorkshire. This courtyard interior – always intended to be mobile, and now available for adoption by other theatres – was arranged on two levels, with red padded bench seating and red scaffolding, grey canvas panels tied onto the tubular poles, creating an intense cockpit atmosphere for a series of tribunal plays in the 1990s: verbatim reconstructions of public inquiries into the sale of arms to Iraq, the Nuremberg trials, the massacre at Srebrenica, the prison for suspected terrorists at Guantanamo Bay and the murder of black schoolboy Stephen Lawrence.

These were subjects of grave national and international concern. But the Tricycle is also a consciously 'local' theatre, providing a focal point for educational activities and participation in what is one of the poorest boroughs in London. An initiative involving recently arrived young migrants and asylum-seekers has moved to the heart of the theatre's operation. When the new Tricycle re-opens, these participants will find a new café with a frontage on the High Road, improved toilets and circulation round the building, a more flexible auditorium – allowing for traverse and in-the-round staging – extra seats (replacing the benches; capacity will rise from 235 to 290) and better sight-lines, all achieved at the cost of

*The distinctive courtyard theatre design was modelled on that of the Georgian Theatre Royal in Richmond, Yorkshire.*

removing the scaffolding that enhanced the courtyard effect.

The Wakefield Tricycle Company was so called in 1972 – by founders Kenneth Chubb and his wife, Shirley Barrie, both Canadian – because it operated out of The Pindar of Wakefield pub in King's Cross. A double play on words invoked the Wakefield Cycle of medieval Mystery Plays, and the fact that Chubb and Barrie were two of the first three sole members. The pub originated in 1517, on another site, when the landlord was one George Green, a former pindar of Wakefield (a pindar was a townsman in charge of impounding stray animals), who, according to a ballad of the day, had fallen in with Robin Hood, Will Scarlett and Little John. When the pub re-opened in its current premises in 1878, it continued its musical and folkloric association – and was also a regular haunt of Karl Marx and Lenin – to the extent that Bob Dylan played his first gig in Britain here in 1962, and The Pogues and Oasis followed, in 1982 and 1994 respectively, with their London debuts. Simultaneously, an 'old time music hall' tradition persisted and in 1992 the pub was renamed The Water Rats in honour of the masonic-style convocation of old-style comedians and light entertainers

known as the Grand Order of Water Rats, who used the place as their administrative headquarters.

Chubb and Barrie joined the new fringe circuit with a programme of new American plays (Sam Shepard was a favourite) and surrealist, experimental French pieces, often visiting other pub venues of the early 1970s such as The Bush in Shepherd's Bush and The King's Head in Islington. Having acquired a lease, and with the support of Brent, the Greater London Council and the Arts Council, Chubb and Barrie got to work on converting the Foresters' Hall and opened for business in 1980. One of their early visiting companies was the Oxford Playhouse with Nicolas Kent's production of *Playboy of the West Indies*, a hilarious Caribbean version of J.M. Synge's Irish classic by Mustapha Matura; and in 1984, Kent succeeded Chubb and Barrie – who returned to Canada – as artistic director.

The whole building was seriously damaged by a fire spreading from a nearby timber yard in the small hours of 21 May 1987. Ironically, the play on the stage was called *Burning Point*, written by a prospective Labour candidate in that

*The famous scaffolded interior is to be replaced and made availabe for adoption by other theatres.*

*The Ira Aldridge dressing room, so named for the black American actor profiled in a Tricycle production.*

year's General Election (in which Tony Blair became Prime Minister) and focusing on an inner city riot; as if to remind us that fire is a traditional danger in the theatre, one burning to the ground every twelve years or so in the late eighteenth and early nineteenth centuries, the Tricycle's companion fringe venue, the Bush, was also damaged by a small conflagration caused by an electrical fault a few weeks later.

The theatre re-opened in 1989, virtually the same, after a successful fundraising campaign and, in 1998, a comfortable 300-seat cinema was added in an extension to the rear, with 'creative space' and offices added for the ever-increasing educational and community work. Kent stood down as artistic director in 2012, concerned about cuts in government spending on the arts in general and on the Tricycle in particular, but his deputy, Indhu Rubasingham, who succeeded him, has maintained the theatre's forward momentum, steering two plays, both of which she directed, into the West End: Lolita Chakrabarti's *Red Velvet*, about the controversial career of the American black actor Ira Aldridge (whose bust is one of several prominently displayed in the Theatre Royal, Drury Lane), and Moira Buffini's *Handbagged*, a playful speculation

on the Queen's weekly 'off-the-record' meetings with Prime Minister Mrs Thatcher in the 1980s, one of a growing sub-genre of contemporary British comedies about the monarchy's relationship with politicians and the society they represent.

Rubasingham's last production before the closure for redevelopment was indicative of both a continuing policy of engaged political drama – American playwright Ayad Akhtar's blistering prison cell thriller, *The Invisible Hand*, outlined the plight of an American banker taken hostage in a Pakistan on the brink of civil riot and financial meltdown – and the new design flexibility, with the set obtruding half-way into the auditorium and the front few rows of benches replaced by seats around the small thrust acting area, the former semblance of a proscenium already obliterated, the courtyard days numbered. The steel structure, largely unscathed in the fire, was adopted in early 2017 by the Valley Park School in Maidstone, Kent, to make a new theatre in the old gymnasium.

Tricycle Theatre

269 Kilburn High Road, London NW6 7JR

www.tricycle.co.uk

# The Other Palace

When the St James Theatre – renamed The Other Palace in early 2017 – opened in September 2012 on the site of the defunct Westminster Theatre, it was the first new purpose-built West End theatre to open since the New London in Drury Lane in 1973. Small and cosy, it seemed nonetheless swallowed up in the extensive development in the Victoria station area. It is part of that development itself, included in a property build as a condition of the lease, with a steeply raked auditorium of 312 seats and a well-appointed 'black box' studio arranged as an L-shaped smaller auditorium around a fixed stage, with a small gallery of sofas and tables to create a cabaret atmosphere. The entrance to the St James is where the Westminster's was, but at ground level (there used to be stairs), next door to the still thriving Phoenix pub, where interval bells for the theatre used to be rung during the thirty years when the Westminster, under the ownership of the Moral Re-Armament organisation, was a 'dry' house, not serving alcohol in the bars.

Bars for the new main house and the studio have made good that dismal characteristic, while a magnificent marble staircase designed by Mark Humphrey, curved and elegant, rises near the entrance to a restaurant serving reasonably priced pre-show dinners. As part of the 2017 relaunch under new management, this restaurant has been redesigned in a comfortable finish of wooden tables and bar stools, an open kitchen serving a variety of tapas sharing dishes. The foyer, too, and the stairway to the downstairs studio space have been tidied up, a display of black and white Hollywood photographs removed and sleek lines restored, in keeping with new digital screens in the box office and by the entrance. The larger space has polished wooden banisters to help you negotiate the steep staircases, and the interiors of both

*The first new purpose-built theatre in London in forty years has 312 seats, an adjustable stage, and is dedicated to new musical theatre.*

*No. 1 dressing room before the show, shared by several actors.*

theatres are fitted out with an attractive, dark wood cladding, good for acoustics but functional in appearance compared to traditional West End plasterwork.

When Andrew Lloyd Webber added the St James to his portfolio of Really Useful Theatre Group venues in December 2015, he proposed the new name for the theatre, The Other Palace, as a statement of intent, and a fresh start. The name jostles up against the Royal Shakespeare Company's The Other Place in Stratford-upon-Avon, and toys with the theatre's location, sandwiched between both Buckingham Palace and the Victoria Palace, lately acquired by Cameron Mackintosh and closed for a £30 million rebuild. Mackintosh is re-opening the VP, as it is known, with the biggest smash hit Broadway musical of recent years, *Hamilton*, while Lloyd Webber's new Other Palace – where Mackintosh's younger brother, Robert, has been an executive producer since it opened – will be a forcing house for new and revived small-scale musical shows, including his own.

In his 'naming of cats' poem, T.S. Eliot opined that a cat must have three different names, and so it was with the St James's. The original St James's Theatre in King Street, behind the Her Majesty's on the other side of St James's Square, was built in 1835, premiered Oscar Wilde's *The Importance of Being Earnest* in 1895, and was closed and demolished – among tremendous protests – in 1957. The new office building on the site, St James's House, had sculptured balcony fronts featured on each floor above the main entrance with four stone bas-relief panels, each composed as a triptych of squares, depicting the heads of the American producer Gilbert Miller,

the actor-manager George Alexander, who ran the St James's for twenty-seven years, Oscar Wilde and the Oliviers – that is, Laurence Olivier and his second wife, Vivien Leigh, who presented seasons at the St James's in the early 1950s – reclining sensuously as Antony and Cleopatra. Luckily, when this building was demolished in the 1980s, and another office building erected on the site, the splendid sculptured friezes were moved to a small alley, Angel Court, running down the side of the building; the Oliviers are right opposite The Golden Lion pub, which has a superb display of programme covers, cast lists and photographs from this period, the other three further down the alley facing up towards King Street.

Before taking that lost theatre's name (without the possessive apostrophe), the original Westminster, on the site of a former chapel, was a cinema from 1924 until it opened in 1931 as a theatre (and was dubbed the Westminster by the managing owner, Amner Hall, an old boy of nearby Westminster School, as indeed is Andrew Lloyd Webber) with *The Anatomist* by James Bridie, directed by Tyrone Guthrie. Throughout the 1930s, the theatre offered a serious and popular repertoire of Ibsen, Shaw, Harley Granville-Barker and J.B. Priestley. The crypt of the chapel provided the bar, dressing rooms and green room for the actors, while the pale grey brickwork of the exterior was complemented by the grey carpeting and pink panelling in the auditorium. At the end of the war, the theatre was managed by Robert Donat (the Oscar-winning star of *Goodbye Mr Chips*), and then Moral Re-Armament got involved in 1946, taking control in 1960 and presenting plays mostly written by MRA director Peter Howard, who was also a journalist and captain of the England rugby team. After Howard's death in 1965, the theatre invited other managements to present plays, but still refused to open the bar for the sale of alcohol.

Respecting the high-minded but often depressingly pious flavour and reputation of the place, producer Bill Kenwright presented, in 1982, a play written in his youth by Pope John Paul II under his real Polish name of Karol Wojtyla. *The Jeweller's Shop*, subtitled 'A meditation on the sacrament of marriage, passing on occasion into a drama', was a play about three couples and their intermingled lives. It did not set the town alight. Most of the building did catch fire, though, in 2002, twelve years after the Westminster finally went dark in 1990. A long campaign led by the Theatres Trust deferred the inevitable demolition until after the fire and resulted in Westminster Council, admittedly in line with a law insisting

on the replacement of one arts facility with another, granting planning permission for a new theatre and studio in 2009. The low-key opening season in September 2012 was launched with *Bully Boy*, a play about combat stress in the Iraq War written by broadcaster and comedian Sandi Toksvig. The newly monikered The Other Palace opened with a 1999 Broadway musical, Michael John LaChiusa's *The Wild Party*, starring Frances Ruffelle, who had played in both the original London staging of Lloyd Webber's *Starlight Express* and Cameron Mackintosh's production (with the Royal Shakespeare Company) of *Les Misérables*.

The Other Palace
12 Palace Street, London SW1E 5JA
www.theotherpalace.co.uk

*A steep rake and good acoustics create a cockpit atmosphere.*

LEGENDS ALIVE

# New Wimbledon Theatre

Wimbledon Theatre, renamed the New Wimbledon by Ambassador Theatre Group when they took over the building in 2004, is the biggest touring and pantomime venue in outer London, with 1,700 seats and some distinctive historic features. Not least of these is the octagonal baroque tower and dome, on which a winged angel once sat above a crystal ball, illuminated by a mercury vapour process throwing out violet rays. The angel, Laetitia, was removed in wartime lest she inadvertently guide the Luftwaffe on their flight path to bomb other theatres in the centre of the city, and was subsequently lost.

The New Wimbledon itself was immune to attack, being in effect a steel and concrete shell designed in 1910 by Cecil Masey, one of the co-designers of the Phoenix Theatre, and Roy Young. It is a landmark building, standing on its own promontory at the top of the Broadway, en route, as it were, to the charming, shack-like Polka Children's Theatre, which opened in a church hall in 1979. The owner was the Irish actor-manager J.B. Mulholland, who installed Turkish baths in the basement for male members only in his acting companies. The entrance foyer is announced with several Corinthian columns, and the theatre opens in a fan shape through the building (104 steps to the top) from a very large, now flat, stage ideal for musicals and dance companies.

There are three galleries with unusual balustraded fronts made of pierced and hammered brass with bronze enrichments, which both hold and reflect the light, and two tiers of bow-fronted boxes, similarly decorated, and described, when the theatre opened, as 'miniature drawing rooms'. There is a spaciousness about the place, especially at the back of the grand circle, where the promenade is decorated with coloured glasswork in a curved wooden screen. The auditorium leaps with painted gods and cherubs, and two muses pose languidly around the royal insignia over the proscenium as if lamenting the fact that the royal charter never came through, even though the seating was originally made of red crocodile skin. With its profusion of marble columns and classical detail, the theatre must once have appeared to resemble a Hollywood setting for a Biblical, or at least Roman, epic.

Wimbledon itself was granted arms in 1906, so the inscription on the crest, 'Sine labe decus' (honour without stain), is included on one of the galleries. And patriotic *amour propre* might have been finally assuaged when the theatre hosted a sixtieth birthday comedy show, *We Are Most Amused*, for the Prince of Wales in 2008, featuring Robin Williams, Bill Bailey, John Cleese, Rowan Atkinson and lashings of the Prince's own Highclere champagne. Laurel and Hardy played a week here after they had participated in the 1947 Royal Variety Performance at the Palladium, while Marlene Dietrich gave one of her last London performances in the early 1970s, as memorialised in a coloured brick display backstage. An even more poignant departure was that of the actor and dramatist Laurence Irving, son of Sir Henry, who performed in his own hit play, *Typhoon*, on the Wimbledon stage before going to a watery grave in 1914 with his wife in the RMS *Empress of Ireland* disaster on the St Lawrence River in North America.

The theatre fell on hard times in the 1960s and was threatened with closure, but a strong local campaign led

*A painted brick on the lower left of a wall backstage commemorates the visit of Marlene Dietrich, among other musicals and comedies of the 1970s.*

to the council buying from the family owners and, after extensive renovation and modernisation, the theatre re-opened in 1968. This period is marked by The Pit saloon (i.e. the stalls bar) portrait of Peter Haddon, who was an actor/manager here from 1955 to 1972. Because of teething troubles, Lionel Bart's *Oliver!* played for three weeks – the stage was big enough to accommodate Sean Kenny's revolutionary, and revolving, designs – in June 1960 before opening at the end of the month at the New Theatre (now the Noël Coward) in the West End. The run was not a success, and the show moved on with few expectations and a slow box office at the New. Eighteen curtain calls on opening night heralded a sensation, the biggest musical theatre hit of the late twentieth century – until Andrew Lloyd Webber came along.

Critics do not visit Wimbledon as regularly as they do the West End, for the simple reason that most touring

shows are West End spin-offs, but they do usually cover the pantomimes. And they arrived in numbers for the first London season of the unique Actors Company in 1974, a troupe led by Ian McKellen and Edward Petherbridge that had completed a UK tour and seasons at the Edinburgh Festival and the Brooklyn Academy in New York. The plays on offer were Chekhov's early draft for *Uncle Vanya*, *The Wood Demon*, Shakespeare's *King Lear* (Robert Eddison as a noble, Biblical Lear and McKellen a brilliant, physically extraordinary Edgar) and Congreve's Restoration masterpiece, *The Way of the World*, updated from eighteenth-century parks and coffee houses to an Edwardian gentlemen's clubland setting.

The idea of the Actors Company, which pre-dated the individual companies instigated by Peter Hall within the National Theatre of the 1980s, and Kenneth Branagh's Renaissance Theatre Company, was that actors were

democratically involved in the production on every level and that everyone would play small roles to prove Stanislavsky's dictum that there are no small parts, only small actors. The joke went around that McKellen, who resolved at an early age only to play big parts, would play Hamlet one night and a waiter the next. 'Oh really, and what is the title of the second play?' 'The Waiter'.

The original decoration of the theatre was in cream and white, rose pink, blue and gold, with much plasterwork and many floral curlicues, creating an Italian opera house effect. There are traces of this still, and a big 1990 renovation saw the Italian painted murals in the auditorium ceiling revived on replacement canvases and a replica of the angel Laetitia restored to her eyrie in the sky. At the end of the 1990s, with the help of Lottery funding, new seating with increased leg-room was added, and the centre aisle removed. The orchestra pit was expanded, a hydraulic forestage

introduced, along with a new grid and counterweight flying system. At the same time, the studio, originally an afternoon tea room and later a dance hall, on the Broadway side of the edifice, returned to the theatre's ownership; it is now a useful fringe address in the capital's theatre ecology. And quite right, too: the sprung maple floor was visited for rehearsals in the 1920s by Adèle and Fred Astaire at the height of their stage fame on either side of the Atlantic.

New Wimbledon Theatre
93 The Broadway, London SW19 1QG
www.atg.co.uk

# Richmond Theatre

A plaster roundel of the actor Edmund Kean in the foyer of the Richmond Theatre is a reminder that Frank Matcham's 1899 attractive and elegant construction continued a deep-rooted local theatre tradition. Kean lived and died – his last words, reputedly, were 'Dying is easy, comedy is hard' – in a house adjoining an earlier Georgian theatre, the Theatre Royal, modelled on Drury Lane, on the other side of Richmond Green, next door to the Tudor palace of Henry VIII and Queen Elizabeth.

Kean had played there several times in his illustrious, convulsive career, and had become the lessee in 1831, two years before he collapsed, while playing Othello at Covent Garden, in the arms of his son, Charles, who was Iago; he was taken home to Richmond. A long funeral procession accompanied him to his burial in St Mary Magdalene parish church in the town centre. Charles placed a stone memorial there in 1839; it's now inside the church, on a wall next to another stone commemoration of the failed actress and popular Victorian novelist, Mary Braddon.

The Theatre Royal was demolished in 1884 and a villa built on the site. Meanwhile, a local hotelier, F.C. Mouflet, opened a small theatre in one of the assembly rooms attached to the Castle Hotel, but the demand outgrew the facility. He therefore hired Matcham to build a new theatre on Little Green, adjacent to the 'main' Green, on a diagonal with Kean's old stomping ground and the palace. The setting is delightful: a border of huge broadleaf trees on all sides of the green, which is owned by the Crown Commission – before cricket arrived, there used to be jousting there in the sixteenth century – the nearby Gate House and Old Palace Yard, the several pubs and restaurants, the easy access to the river. The holiday atmosphere of all this seeps into

*One of Frank Matcham's most beautiful theatres has distinctive plasterwork and a marble veneer proscenium stage flanked by decorated columns.*

LEFT *A memorial plaque to the architect on the frontage, above the foundation stone laid by Mrs Mouflet in 1898.*

OPPOSITE *The original gas-powered sun-burner in the auditorium, surrounded by plasterwork scenes from Shakespeare.*

OVERLEAF *The perfectly proportioned theatre, warm and welcoming, is ideal for pantomime.*

the red brick and terracotta façade, the beautiful frontage and indeed, one feels, the actors and audiences.

Matcham often designed thematically. In the Richmond Theatre, with a nod to the palace across the Green, he combines elegance with exuberance in an 'Elizabethan' style. Outside, you are welcomed by the rising figure of Euterpe, the muse of lyric poetry with her lute. A baroque centrepiece maintains a lovely equilibrium between the tall twin towers with green copper cupolas and an arched entrance with flower pots, stained glass, extant stone inscriptions for the Pit and the Gallery entrances and a perfectly proportioned small stairway with balustrades. Inside, the ceiling in the auditorium has painted panels from four Shakespearean plays – *Hamlet*, *A Midsummer Night's Dream*, *King Lear* and *Romeo and Juliet* – and, above the imposing marble veneer proscenium, flanked by elaborately decorated columns bearing figures of Tragedy

and Comedy, a quotation from Pope's prologue to Addison's *Cato*: 'To wake the soul by tender strokes of art.'

The place was built, very quickly, in one year at a cost of £30,000, well over the going rate of £20,000 at that time, and opened, suitably enough, with the Ben Greet company in Shakespeare's Elizabethan comedy of romantic love and rural escape, *As You Like It*. The theatre was fully electric from the start, with its own steam generator supplying over a thousand lamps. There was a refurbishment in 1915 and further work in 1975 – when the foyer was restored and the rude gallery reseated as an upper circle – but the major changes and renewals were made during a two-year closure from 1989, with a new extension to the right of the main entrance (the red brickwork is a sympathetic match with the original) making room for a new box office, a new stalls long bar and, above them, some light-filled offices. The central aisle in the stalls was removed, the original stalls bar converted into toilets, and a tented entrance canopy unwisely added in the 1960s consigned at last to the rubbish dump; the historian John Earl caught the mood when he said that this 'self-conscious' carbuncle 'should be removed to the accompaniment of dancing in the streets'.

The interior decorative work was done by the designer Carl Toms. His assistant, Lawrence Llewelyn-Bowen, painted a witty and symbolic history of the theatre on the ceiling of the restored entrance vestibule. This shows

nymphs and cherubs helping Pallas Athene to expel Father Time from the Theatre while another group of nymphs and cherubs bring a memorial tablet of Frank Matcham to the enthroned figure of the Borough of Richmond. The handsome entrance wooden doors, and the small Victorian ticket booths, are made of mahogany; there's a lot of polished mahogany throughout, not least in the dress circle, where a long curved rail is decorated with brass finials, resembling small-scale capstans, at either end, and in the dress circle bar, a particularly attractive room with access to small balconies on the front. A small room leading off the circle bar is currently dedicated to Norman Fenner, the civil servant, amateur set designer and Matcham specialist who was also the theatre's volunteer archivist, spending his retirement compiling a record of every Richmond production since the theatre opened, and conducting tours of the theatre.

Only Fenner's room has the distinctive light green decorative finish of Matcham's original, though you sense something of that among the cherubs and floral plasterwork along the frontages of the circles. Otherwise, Toms went down the familiar red paint and velvet route in the auditorium, but it's stylishly done. This really is a 'warm' theatre, whether you are watching one of the many pre- or post-West End touring shows – the stage is not really equipped for large musicals – or the ever-popular pantomime, when the summery airiness of the place is transformed, with a shake of glittering fairy dust, into a glorious crucible of festive high spirits.

Richmond Theatre
Little Green, Richmond TW9 1QJ
www.atg.co.uk

# Playhouse Theatre

The Playhouse is a lovely intimate medium-sized theatre, seating around 750 people, curvilinear and feminine, known to its technical staff as 'Thalia', the Greek muse whose name, and statues, adorn the proscenium. But she's had a chequered past: an avalanche of masonry from Charing Cross station killed six people on the stage during the 1906 rebuild; periods of closure and uncertainty; even a brief ownership by the novelist and former politician Jeffrey Archer, who sold off some of the dressing rooms for office development and rentals; and an extended term as a significant home of BBC radio entertainment, broadcasting live in the 1950s, with an audience, both *The Goon Show* and *Hancock's Half Hour*.

It is thought that the theatre builder and manager Sefton Parry constructed the Royal Avenue Theatre, as it was first known, in 1882, to designs by F.H. Fowler and Hill, in order to make a fast buck from South Eastern Railway who were planning to extend Charing Cross station into that site. But this never happened and the 1,200-seat house, facing Platform 6, pressed up against a station entrance, and, giving on to the Embankment on the Northumberland Avenue side, opened with an Offenbach operetta. It seems an ideal location but the theatre has never shaken off a sense of being 'off the beaten track', even though Villiers Street round the corner, leading up the Strand, is a-bustle with shops, pubs and one of the best wine bars in London. The policy altered with one of George Alexander's first forays into management before he went on to run the St James's and produce Oscar Wilde. Bernard Shaw had his first West End hit with *Arms and the Man* in 1894. It was under Cyril Maude's management in 1905 that the changes to the auditorium were initiated. The fatal accident delayed the opening of the new Playhouse until 1907,

*An enchanted atmosphere of curved balustrades, Victorian street lamps, statues to Thalia and equine skulls.*

*Flywheels for the pit lift under the stage reinforce the idea of the theatre as a ship.*

Maude having received a record £20,000 in compensation from South Eastern Railways.

The elevation in Portland style was the same as in the original, and remains so today, but without the ornamental carvings and the statues, including one of Shakespeare, between the figures of Comedy and Tragedy over the main entrance. The French Renaissance style continued inside the remodelled horseshoe auditorium, where the seating capacity was reduced to around 750: the new intimacy was enhanced by flowing curves, unusually plain and elegant balustrading on the two balconies, unfussy plasterwork and medallion portraits of poets of all nations. This was the work of Detmar Blow (whose grandson was married to the fashion stylist, Isabella Blow) and the French architect Fernand Billerey. Thalia, almost life-size, appears in the stage boxes, supported by caryatids, as well as over the proscenium flanked by ornately winged angels.

Most extraordinary of all are two features unique to this theatre: four Victorian lamp-posts, identical to those on Northumberland Avenue, stand proudly, two each side, on the circle boxes; and around the stalls are eight identical gilded equine skulls, all of them representing Bucephalus, the horse of Alexander the Great. In these early years, the auditorium was decorated in carton-pierre, a sort of papier-mâché stiffened with plaster, its colour scheme ivory and gold, and you can see traces of this Gallic gleam in the foyer still, in the mirrors, black and white marble floor (though that is, perhaps, rather more Edwardian) and two magnificent light fittings, a 'cabbage' chandelier (the light nestling in a brass, leafy-looking basket) and a rhomboid glass-encased light suspended by hefty brass prongs and known as 'the champagne bucket'.

A pair of simple iron gates on either side of the foyer lead to the stairs up to the circle (stage and stalls are at street level) where two huge, dark Shakespearean canvases glower on either side and continue into the upper circle; this second balcony pierces the heart of each painting, as though stabbing them with their balustrades; at some stage the paintings have been dull-glazed, so they cannot be restored to reveal

*The still-working thunderball run, with weights and ropes, demonstrated on theatre tours, but not in productions.*

the identity of each play represented, though the one on the auditorium left is probably our old friend *A Midsummer Night's Dream*. The same treatment has been served on all the paintings, roundels and the circular dome in the ceiling. This is one of the first free-standing theatres, the first in London with fully cantilevered balconies and, ticking the modern Health and Safety boxes, there are no more than five steps at any access or exit point.

Between the wars, Gladys Cooper starred in several plays by Somerset Maugham and shared the management with Frank Curzon before succeeding him as sole lessee in 1927, presenting plays with another great actor-manager, Gerald du Maurier, father of novelist Daphne. But there was nothing smooth or continuous about the Playhouse's operation, always bedevilled by being 'off the map'. Nancy Price ran her People's National Theatre for a couple of seasons in 1938/9 but several years of closure followed until it re-opened again during the war, in 1942, with a revival of Maugham's *Home and Beauty*. The programme was now a complete mix of plays,

revues and ballet seasons. Thora Hird starred in Agatha Christie's *Murder at the Vicarage* in 1949. During the war, the BBC had broadcast to the French Resistance from here, and they returned in 1951 – staying until 1975 – to broadcast the Goons, Hancock and many others. The theatre was often used for pop and rock broadcast gigs, especially during a dispute in the 1960s between the BBC and record companies over 'Needle-time'; the groups, including The Who, The Rolling Stones and The Beatles, recorded at the Playhouse so that their music could be broadcast on the radio without having to pay out to the record companies.

Even during the years of closure that followed the BBC's residency, the rock music connection persisted, and Queen made one of their most celebrated videos, 'It's a Kind of Magic', here, gaining much purchase on the state of dilapidation and disrepair that was all around. The video does have a close-up, though, of the stucco cameo of Cyril Maude's son, John, in the foyer, his face one of sinister ambiguity; theatre lore decreed that when he looked as though he was smiling, the

*The original thunder run with cannon balls, ready for action.*

*The second balustraded balcony pierces the dark Shakespearean canvas in the curvilinear, 'feminine' auditorium.*

show was a hit. If not, not. Anyway, John's face is hidden for the immediate future behind the redecoration and restoration that began in earnest in 1987 when the theatre was acquired by entrepreneur Robin Gonshaw, who built a set of offices, Aria House, on the top, removing all last trace of the statuary but in no way compromising the scenic flying facilities. The first new show was Howard Goodall's musical *Girl Friends*.

The 1882 auditorium had drapery, curtains and seats of red damask, and the 1987 refurbishment returned to that colour scheme, by-passing the oranges and browns of the 1907 vintage. The panelled walls are hung with a design based on Napoleon's cloak, a myriad bees (each bee is like an inverted fleur-de-lys) swarming in regimented patterns through the theatre, and across the carpeting, too. One important aspect of the 1987 work was the repair and fine-tuning of the wooden sub-stage. The stage machinery there is second only in importance to that of Her Majesty's, and it's all in good working order, even if unused (this is because you cannot insure the hemp ropes). Here again, aboard 'Thalia', the historical idea of a theatre as a ship – with its crew, rigging, decks and cannon

balls for the famous thunder run – is reinforced. Seamen used to be stage hands and in fact Playhouse papers show that technicians here were paid in money and a tot of rum.

The theatre has changed hands several times in the past thirty years, hosting the Peter Hall company in a series of classics, a Ray Cooney farce and a season of the Almeida in the West End in 1998 which featured Liam Neeson as Oscar Wilde in David Hare's *The Judas Kiss* and a fully clothed Juliette Binoche in Pirandello's *Naked*. The National Theatre's long-running revival of J.B. Priestley's *An Inspector Calls*, directed by Stephen Daldry, also paid an extended visit. Oddly, there was briefly a tapas bar in the downstairs stalls bar. Ambassador Theatre Group, involved for some years, now owns the Playhouse outright and has instigated its own front-of-house renovation programme with new shiny bars and comfy sofas in their VIP lounge.

Playhouse Theatre

Northumberland Avenue, London WC2N 5DE

www.playhousetheatrelondon.com

# Adelphi Theatre

We think of the 1,500-seat Adelphi on the Strand, with its Art Deco frontage and strikingly angular, unfussy auditorium, set well back from the front entrance, as a modern sort of place. In many ways it is; today's Adelphi is more or less the same as it was in the rebuild of 1930, though without, alas, rose-coloured doors, chrome-plated grilles and Lalique fountain lights. But of all London theatres, the Adelphi has the bittiest and most volatile architectural history. Today's is the fourth theatre on this same site bounded by narrow Bull Inn Court to the side and Maiden Lane to the rear.

The first was built in 1806 by a man who had made a fortune from inventing a blue washing powder and whose daughter fancied a singing career. The opening programme, *Miss Scott's Entertainment*, was a solo show, given by Jane Scott, of songs, recitations and impersonations. She was also the manager, and the performance ended with fireworks. Melodramas followed, and it's a fact that both musical theatre and melodrama featured conspicuously here for two centuries. Nothing remains of the Sans Pareil, as the theatre was first christened, except the basic ground plan. In 1819, John Scott sold on the Adelphi, as it became known; the three Adam brothers (*adelphoi* is Greek for 'brothers') had built Adelphi Terrace and John Adam Street across the road on the Embankment side at the end of the eighteenth century. In 1822, a play called *Tom and Jerry* – not a cat and mouse game, but a tale of two men-about-town – was the first in Britain to play for one hundred consecutive performances. The theatre boasted the first 'sinking stage' in 1834, and architect Samuel Beazley provided a new arched and handsomely inset façade in 1840, by which time the Adelphi was acknowledged as the most fashionably attended theatre in town. Dramatic versions of Dickens were popular. The auditorium was altered in 1848, but the third major rebuild in 1858 – coinciding with the opening of the Royal Opera House – claimed the title of grandest, most spacious and beautiful commercial theatre in London; the front of the main balcony, backed by private boxes and cantilevered out from wrought-iron trusses, was left open so that ladies' dresses could be seen.

The Gatti family, who had figured so prominently in the story of the music hall under the arches at Charing Cross, took over the theatre in 1879 and by 1887 had extended across the theatre building right up against Bull Inn Court and opened the Adelphi Theatre Restaurant on the ground floor; this right-hand third of the building (as you face it from the Strand) has long since reverted to non-theatrical ownership, and the Gattis' restaurant has most recently been recast as an amusement arcade and a burger joint.

A royal entrance on Maiden Lane, opposite Rule's, London's oldest restaurant, led to a 90-foot corridor on the stage right side of the theatre through to the royal box and anteroom. It was by this door that, on 16 December 1897, the popular, dashing matinée idol of the melodrama, William Terriss (father of Ellaline Terriss, the musical comedy actress who married the actor-manager Seymour Hicks), was murdered aged fifty. Although the stage door at that time was in Bull Inn Court, Terriss had a key to a pass door next to the royal entrance which opened directly into the dressing rooms. As he fumbled for the key, he was attacked by Richard Arthur Prince, a disgruntled small-part actor who felt he had been insulted by him when Terriss had in fact tried to help; Prince was destitute and drunk, and had

been forcibly ejected from the Vaudeville Theatre next door. He stabbed Terriss twice in the back and a third time in the chest. Terriss died within the hour on his dressing room sofa. At the Old Bailey, Prince's defence entered a plea of insanity and he was sent to Broadmoor where he organised entertainments for the inmates and led the orchestra until his death in 1936, aged seventy-one. Henry Irving, the first actor to be knighted, two years earlier in 1895, reflected bluntly on the still pervasive lack of respect for his profession and the furore over Prince's sentence: 'Terriss was an actor, so his murderer will not be executed.'

In the first decade of the twentieth century, the Royal Adelphi (so named between 1902–40) was renowned for Shakespeare and poetic drama, but that all changed under the management of musical comedy producer George Edwardes in 1908. A string of popular hits was followed by Gladys Cooper in *Peter Pan* in 1923, revues with Jack Hulbert and Cecily Courtneidge, and the delightful Vivian Ellis musical *Mr Cinders* in 1929. The complete rebuild for the Gattis in 1930, designed by Ernest Schaufelberg (who had designed the Fortune Theatre opposite Drury Lane in 1924 with a lovely nude sculpture on the side of it), was remarkable for the flat frontage in white faience tiles on a black base, with decoration, and the rectilinear auditorium of red seating and wood finishing; it was conceived in straight lines, with the angle of 32 degrees the master note, and a colour scheme of orange, green and gold with bronze insets on the underside of the two circles. The foyer made an Art Deco virtue of its length, with lozenge-shaped coloured lights in the ceiling. The opening show was Rodgers and Hart's *Ever Green* starring Jessie Matthews ('Dancing on the Ceiling' used London's first revolving stage), and Vivian Ellis returned with another hit, *Bless the Bride*, in 1947; when the theatre was extensively renovated in 1993, new celebratory bars were dedicated to both Matthews and Ellis, one at the back of the stalls, one at the front. Marie Tempest gave her farewell performance in 1940 and Jack Hylton presented a series of variety shows in the 1950s.

*The Adelphi has long been an ideal, popular home for musicals, from Vivian Ellis to Sondheim and Lloyd Webber.*

*View from the fly floor, looking down onto the stage with the safety curtain 'in'.*

The Gattis finally sold out to Woolworth's in 1955, but permission to turn the place, including the restaurant, into a store, was refused and the London County Council finally put a stop to any further office redevelopment plans. The venue continued to be a prime musical theatre house, hosting *The Music Man* (the show that beat *West Side Story* to a best musical Tony) in 1961; the long-running – over five years – *Charlie Girl* (in which, said the critic Kenneth Tynan, Anna Neagle shook her voice at the audience like a tiny fist) in 1965; and, in the 1970s, revivals of *Show Boat* and *The King and I* and the London premiere of Stephen Sondheim and Hugh Wheeler's *A Little Night Music* with Joss Ackland, Jean Simmons, Hermione Gingold and Liz Robertson. Robertson returned to the theatre in 1979 in *My Fair Lady*, two years before she married the show's lyricist Alan Jay Lerner. She was his eighth, and final, wife. Lerner loved women and possessed, he said, the bills to prove it.

Stephen Fry's hugely successful rejig of *Me and My Girl*, the 1937 'Lambeth Walk' musical, starring Robert Lindsay and Emma Thompson, was another long-running hit.

Ownership passed eventually to a partnership of New York producer James Nederlander and Andrew Lloyd Webber's Really Useful Theatre Group. In the 1993 renovation – completed in order to open with Lloyd Webber's *Sunset Boulevard* (book and lyrics by Don Black and Christopher Hampton) – many of the 1930 features are retained, or at least alluded to, in the public areas. The seating is once again red, the bust of Charles B. Cochran, the great producer and manager who ran the Adelphi in the 1920s and 1930s, sits proudly in the upper circle area, while the slightly cramped circle bar, decorated, as are all the corridors, in salmon pink, has the most beautiful coloured window and Art Deco mirror. It is typical of the Adelphi's no-nonsense style that the royal box, with no crest or lettering, is indistinguishable from the other three boxes, though it does have a retiring room behind.

Adelphi Theatre

Strand, London WC2R 0NS

www.reallyusefultheatres.co.uk

# Queen's Theatre

Because of the complete destruction of the front of the theatre and the back of the circles during one night's bombing in September 1940, you'd never tell from the pavement on Shaftesbury Avenue that the Queen's is a Siamese twin – joined at the hip by a block of offices and a ground floor restaurant – of the glorious Globe (now the Gielgud). But W.G.R. Sprague's restructured Queen's shares many decorative delights inside with its other half, and the 1959 accretions by Festival of Britain architect Hugh Casson have been unapologetically sustained in the modern era; the venue had been dark and derelict for twenty years, re-opening with John Gielgud's Shakespearean solo show, *The Seven Ages of Man*.

Casson's glass curtain wall wrapped around the cylindrical conjunction of Shaftesbury Avenue and Wardour Street was described by historian John Earl as 'an architectural gate-crasher wearing the wrong suit to the party', but in a way the sheer Modernist nerve of what he did undermines such objections, though you do entertain a few doubts as you penetrate the rather awkwardly arranged foyer. The glass doors on the street, though, have some fine old heavy brass door-handles in the shape of theatrical masks. There's a glass fibre-optic chandelier, and a second one in the 'new' circle bar which has a distinctly 1950s wooden finish and furnishings, with a one-way panoramic view along Shaftesbury Avenue (from the outside, there's currently a magically applied giant poster image of *Les Misérables*, the musical that transferred here from the Barbican and the Palace, and is now an immovable West End fixture in its fourth decade).

On the stairs is affixed a large pair of wings fashioned from Cornish tin seemingly sprouting from the laconic seated photographic image of Noël Coward; they come from his sitting room in Les Avants and signify his association with this theatre.

*A new chandelier and muses keep watch over the handsomely redecorated Queen's Theatre auditorium with its exuberant plasterwork and panels of striped wallpaper.*

*The Jacob's ladder to the fly floor offers a crepuscular vision backstage.*

*The oval saucer dome in the ceiling, with a glimpse of the upper gallery.*

He appeared at the Queen's after a long absence from the West End in 1966 in his own *Suite in Three Keys* and, in the year before he died, in 1972, Maggie Smith and Robert Stephens played in *Private Lives* as their marriage was falling apart and the strain telling in the performance. Coward went backstage and wagged his finger at Smith for overdoing it: 'You've got very common indeed. You're almost as common as Gertie.' Smith later told Alan Bennett that to be compared with Gertrude Lawrence (who had played the original Amanda Prynne opposite Coward himself), if only for overdoing it, seemed such a compliment that she instantly mended her ways. All the same, Smith's Amanda was an unforgettable performance as indeed was her later Queen's Theatre *tour de force* as Miss Shepherd in Alan Bennett's *The Lady in the Van*. A tiny hospitality room at the back of the dress circle carries her name. This hidey-hole is considerably less plush than the Marlene Room at the side of the stalls (Marlene Dietrich played a season here in 1972, the same year as Maggie's *Private Lives*, which moved next door to the Globe), decorated in green and grey striped wallpaper and come-hither photos of the chanteuse.

At the top, in the upper circle bar, there are Angus McBean portraits of other Queen's alumni, including Celia Johnson, Peggy Ashcroft and Gwen Ffrangcon-Davies. But it's Gielgud who is most deep-dyed in the theatre's history. He made his West End debut here as a twenty-five-year-old Hamlet (from the Old Vic) in 1930 and in 1937 followed just twelve performances in Emlyn Williams' *He Was Born Gay* with an astonishing eight-month season of four plays – *Richard II*, *The Merchant of Venice*, *Three Sisters* and *The School for Scandal* – playing the lead in each one and returning in 1938, opposite

Marie Tempest, in Dodie Smith's *Dear Octopus*.

The cream and gold of the original décor by Waring and Gillow was restored by Casson in 1959 with an additional element of red, and most of the Italianate plaster details preserved. The *putti* on the front of the circles are particularly fat and fulsome, frolicking among ferns and flowers like children splashing around in a paddling pool, and the upper boxes are set off handsomely between square Corinthian columns supporting an entablature and an arch. The ceiling is an oval saucer dome with four semi-circular blue half-moons, each guarded with pairs of bare-breasted muses. The Really Useful Group Theatres (and Bridgepoint Capital, formerly NatWest Equity) bought the lease from Stoll Moss in 2000 before the freehold was acquired by Delfont Mackintosh in 2002, along with the rest of the 'island' site bounded by the Gielgud on Rupert Street, Winnet Street at the back and Wardour Street, in 2006. In a 2010 refurbishment, there was a major overhaul of the flooring, toilets and foyer bar. The centre aisle was removed (increasing the capacity to well over 1,000) and red seats and a new chandelier installed. The latest construction project, tricky in such a constricted and congested area, is the provision of more dressing rooms and showers backstage and the complete removal of a curved wall to make the wing space much bigger. It used to be said that these old West End theatres were no longer fit for purpose. The mood has changed, and the investment in their future is picking up pace.

Queen's Theatre
51 Shaftesbury Avenue, London W1D 6BA
www.queenstheatre.co.uk

*The fly floor, where scenes are changed with all hands on deck.*

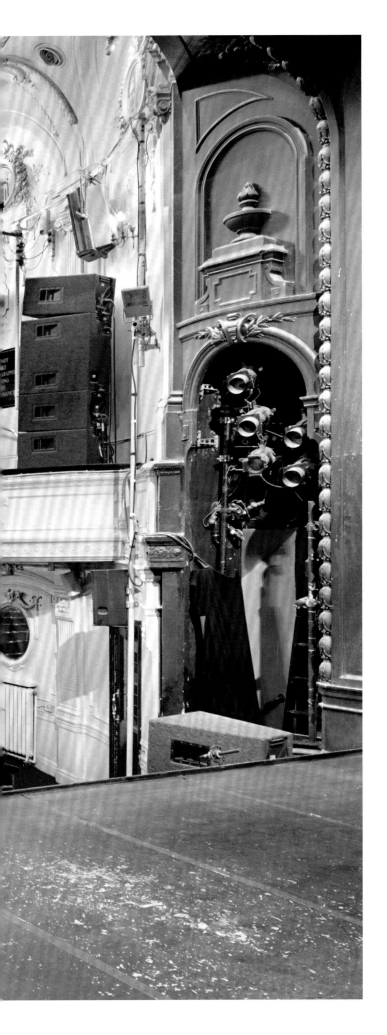

# Ambassadors Theatre

The Ambassadors, one of the most famous of theatres on account of being the origin and first home of the longest-running play in the world, Agatha Christie's *The Mousetrap*, was bought by the unrelated Ambassador Theatre Group in 1999 and renamed, mysteriously, the New Ambassadors, which it isn't. It is palpably the 'old' Ambassadors, rather run-down and unloved inside – except, of course, by the people who work there – and it's in dressed-down limbo, awaiting the outcome of a local council decision on the plans of Cameron Mackintosh, who bought the theatre in 2014, to completely revamp the interior as a new 450-seat musicals and cabaret venue named The Sondheim.

The Ambassadors, designed by W.G.R. Sprague in 1913 as one of a pair with the St Martin's – both were separate financial enterprises; the very different St Martin's next door is where *The Mousetrap* moved in 1974 when the long lease on the Ambassadors, owned by its producer, Peter Saunders, ran out – is described by the Theatres Trust as his most striking feat of compression. It is one of the smallest West End theatres, and it feels like it. But that is because the interior, bars and facilities have been so muddled up. Only the eight ambassadorial crests around the auditorium front ceiling – they were painted out in 1914 for political reasons on the outbreak of war and were reinstated in 1958 – really imply the original elegance; these, and other plasterwork in the Grade II-listed theatre, would be removed and stored in the new Sondheim Theatre.

With its restrained classical exterior, elegant auditorium of violet, ivory and gold, horseshoe balcony and raised tier at the rear, this theatre was once a natural home for the first intimate revues in London, starting with the French singer Alice Delysia

*One of the smallest West End theatres, the Ambassadors was the home of intimate revue, and the world's longest-running play, The Mousetrap.*

*Agatha Christie's 'thank you' present to the theatre for presenting her thriller is on show in the foyer.*

in *Odds and Ends* presented by Charles B. Cochran in 1914. Ivor Novello and Hermione Gingold made their debuts here in 1921, Paul Robeson appeared in Eugene O'Neill's *The Emperor Jones* in 1925 and the gruesome thriller *Rope* made Patrick (*Gaslight*) Hamilton's name in 1929. There was a second wave of revues in the war, most of them starring Gingold. After the war, and until Peter Saunders acquired the lease, there was a mixed programme including Peter Brook's 1949 production of *Dark of the Moon*, the Broadway spiritualist folk drama based on the ballad of Barbara Allen and the witch boy. Christie's *The Mousetrap*, originally called 'Three Blind Mice', opened on 25 November 1952 and ran until 25 March 1974, the cast led by Richard Attenborough as Detective Sergeant Trotter for two years, with his wife, Sheila Sim, staying for the first six months as Mollie Ralston. On its twenty-first birthday in November 1973, the whodunnit became the longest-running play in stage history.

From the moment Ray Cooney took out a three-year lease, there was always talk of the theatre becoming a commercial outpost for the fringe and other companies,

and that is what happened, though without any coherent policy. Christopher Hampton's adaptation of *Les Liaisons Dangereuses*, starring Alan Rickman and Lindsay Duncan, was a game-changer, running for four years after it transferred from the Royal Shakespeare Company in 1986. Ten years later, the Royal Court – while their own Sloane Square headquarters was being overhauled – leased the premises and 'vandalised' the venue, knocking off the plasterwork and creating two 'fringe' theatres; the circle was extended across the stalls, and the stalls level downstairs altered into a bar and studio space.

These ravages have left the theatre reeling, though ATG presented some quality shows – John Hurt in Beckett's *Krapp's Last Tape* and the delightful Irish two-hander *Stones in His Pockets* among them – before ownership was assumed in 2014 by Stephen Waley-Cohen, who had been nominated by Saunders as his successor at Mousetrap Productions in 1994, licensing the play on behalf of Christie's grandson, Mathew Prichard, to whom, as a boy, she had gifted the rights before the play even opened.

Somewhat dispiritingly, the phenomenal percussion show, *Stomp* – which proves that drumming is as much a matter of dustbin lids, bovver boots, kitchen utensils and body parts as it is of skins, canvas and tympani, maybe more so – has been playing for half the week since 2007, with other companies, including the National Youth Theatre in the summer months, filling in.

The red brick and stucco façade now seems to proclaim a theatre in denial of its own history and architectural distinction. Some theatre-goers and even theatre artists may think that this is a good thing, an acknowledgement of the West End's 'irrelevance' to them. But audiences don't think like that. They want to see their serious and challenging dramas, as well as their thrillers and revues,

in a more amenable setting. Opposite the Ambassadors, and the St Martin's, on West Street, is the Ivy, a restaurant particularly associated with the theatre and a haven for West End stars from Noël Coward and Laurence Olivier to Judi Dench and Kenneth Branagh. Lately revamped under the new ownership of billionaire entrepreneur Richard Caring, the Ivy remains a theatrical mecca, full of atmosphere, theatrical expectations and artwork by Damien Hirst, as if daring the 'old' Ambassadors to reinvent itself once again, and some time very soon.

Ambassadors Theatre

West Street, London WC2H 9ND

www.theambassadorstheatre.co.uk

*The fly floor, hempen ropes and wires all tidy and ship-shape, lighting bars below to the right.*

HIDDEN GEMS

# Normansfield
# Theatre

Normansfield is not an operating theatre, although it is set in the grounds of a former hospital. But the beguiling auditorium, a gem of a 'lost' Victorian small playhouse, is still used for concerts and musical hall evenings and by small opera companies, especially so since the premises have been secured within the surrounding housing development and its collection of old stock painted Victorian scenery – acknowledged as the finest in the country – preserved with help from the Heritage Lottery Fund in 2015.

The theatre nestles unassumingly in the grounds of Langdon Park, ten minutes' walk from Hampton Wick station along the Kingston Road in Teddington, its institutional exterior of grey stone, tiles and brickwork scarcely hinting at the treasures within. The auditorium, the size of a small football pitch, has a high, beamed roof of pine from which hangs a fully restored steel sun-burner, originally a source of both light and ventilation. There's an Arts and Crafts feeling about the place: painted panels of birds and wild flowers on either side of the toy-theatre-like proscenium, with paintings of Tragedy, Comedy, Painting and Music. The brick walls are decorated with wrought-ironwork, gothic arcading and life-sized paintings of the inhabited costumes designed for Gilbert and Sullivan's *Ruddigore* at the Savoy in 1887. The ironwork is realised in full decorative glory along the front of the balcony as the focus of attention moves to the pocket-sized stage, where the grooves for the scenery are still in working order, though not often used. A recent production of *Carmen*, for instance, was played out under simply suggested Andalusian arches with an arbitrary cloth of domestic buildings behind.

The place was built in 1879 for the recreation, entertainment and therapeutic instruction of his patients by a pioneering

*The steel sun-burner hangs from a high-beamed roof of well-preserved pine.*

*The theatre's collection of painted Victorian scenery is the finest in Britain.*

physician called John Langdon Down. He and his wife, Mary, had founded the hospital in 1868 as a private facility for people with what we now call 'learning disabilities', and other psychological disturbances and conditions. A proportion of these people, some of whom were also referred to as 'students', were Down's syndrome patients – the doctor's name stuck to the diagnosis – and all of them were engaged not only in the life of the theatre, but in woodwork and farming projects, excursions to the hospital's boathouse on the river and further afield to holiday breaks in Ramsgate in Kent. The designer of the theatre was Rowland Plumbe – not known to have designed any other theatre – who had a relative in Earlswood Asylum for Idiots (this was the standard early Victorian classification for the 'mentally subnormal' or 'feeble-minded' or indeed 'Mongoloids') in Surrey, the institution where Langdon Down had been appointed medical superintendent in 1858, before establishing his own, more radically enlightened *modus operandi* in Normansfield.

The hospital was taken over by the National Health Service in 1951, and closed in 1997, since when the fate of the theatre has been in the balance. But from the 1980s onwards, there has been much expert interest in the place, not least because of the scenery cache. This section of the old hospital, always known as the theatre wing, and part of Langdon Down's former house, was handed over to the Langdon Down Centre Trust in a planning agreement with the builders. The Trust merged with the Down's Syndrome Association in 2010.

Many ornate fixtures and fittings in the Grade II listed theatre are stored, as well as the scenery. The painted panels have been attributed to Marianne North, the Victorian biologist and botanical artist who is commemorated in a gallery in Kew Gardens. A museum in other parts of the building, now open to the public and to school tours, charts the work of Langdon Down in both Normansfield and Earlswood, and focuses on some individual case histories and the theatre, which always accommodated amateur performances from the beginning. The painted scenery on the stage is a replica of the now dangerously fragile original scenery. The project to protect this scenery started with external draining works and continued in photographing and cataloguing every item – backdrops, borders, additional flats and stand-alone pieces of scenery – creating a digital archive of immense historical interest.

The result is a 'virtual theatre' existing alongside its own ghost-like, weirdly atmospheric blueprint. It was ironically appropriate, therefore, that the *Carmen* in question was accompanied by a 'virtual orchestra', a computer-generated synthesiser capable of adjusting to dynamics and tempi in performance as controlled by a musical director with one hand while he gestured to the actors with the other, seated at a small desk on the floor in front of the stage. The absence of quite a few patrons after the interval suggested that, before too long, there would be a 'virtual audience', too, but somehow this possibility seemed not too outlandish in a hall so resonant with poignant and magical echoes of its own history.

Normansfield Theatre

2A Langdon Park, Middlesex TW11 9PS

www.langdondowncentre.org.uk

*The wrought iron and painted panels – attributed to Victorian biologist Marianne North – lend an Arts and Crafts feeling.*

# Alexandra Palace Theatre

Alexandra Palace, built high on a hill in 196 acres of parkland in north London as a 'people's palace', opened on 24 May 1873. Its huge iron frame, formerly housing the 1862 International Exhibition, was transported from South Kensington to the gracious greenery of Muswell Hill. Just sixteen days and 124,000 visitors later, the emporium was destroyed by fire. Nothing daunted, the powers that be set about rebuilding it immediately and the new palace opened on 1 May 1875. This time a theatre was included seating 2,500 people.

It is this theatre – more of a mid-nineteenth-century music hall, and closed to audiences for over eighty years – that is at the heart of an exciting project that will restore not only the theatre (with a new capacity of 1,300 people) to everyday use but also re-animate the former BBC studios as an interactive visitor attraction, and the handsome East Court that sits imposingly between them as a welcoming community area complete with a new foyer for the theatre, a café and a bar at the back of the theatre stalls. The East Court is to the right-hand side of the main Great Hall entrance as you face the palace, and will become a destination in its own right. The magnificent Great Hall, which in 1875 housed the Henry Willis organ, in its day one of the largest in Europe, has a capacity of thousands, and continues as a venue for rock concerts, beer festivals, garden shows, sporting events and farmers' markets, and the indoor ice rink is one of the largest and most popular in London.

So the new theatre should help enliven one of the most ambitious, and architecturally significant, entertainment complexes in the country. And that is what Alexandra Palace always was: with sculpture and painting exhibitions, a museum

*The heavily moulded ceiling and pink, peeling walls of this 1875 music hall date from 1919 and will be left as they are in the renovation. The shallow circle is dimly visible from the stage.*

*An inset statue decorates the perfectly proportioned proscenium.*

and lecture hall, library, banqueting rooms, a 3,500-seat concert room (subsequently a roller-skating rink, then an ice rink) and, in the parkland around, a racetrack and trotting ring, cricket pitch, ornamental lakes and a funfair. Of most historical significance, and the main argument for its Grade II listing, was the theatre which, as the Theatre Trusts much later reported, 'demonstrates a transition between an archaic system of scene-handling – grooves and drum-and-shaft flying gear – to the modern system of counter-weighted flying'. Also, the mechanical timber under the stage is the last surviving machinery of its kind in its original state, and will be so preserved as an academic resource and visitor attraction.

The popularity of the palace and its facilities continued to the end of the nineteenth century when, after running into financial difficulties, an Act of Parliament in 1901 created the Alexandra Palace and Park Trust, to be administered by the local authorities. In the same year, the theatre was appropriated for use as a cinema. In 1907, its second balcony

was removed – you can see the scars in the stripped-back walls, which will remain thus after the renovation – and the fire staircases were built. On the outbreak of war in 1914, the whole palace, including the theatre, was requisitioned by the government first as a Belgian refugee camp and later as a German and Austrian internment camp for the duration.

In 1919, after the war, the producer, historian and sometime critic William Macqueen-Pope was appointed theatre manager and transformed the auditorium into something very similar to its present (though more dilapidated) condition, installing a heavily moulded ceiling with a fleur-de-lys stencilled pattern on the roundel that is still visible. There were two arched and decorated doorways on each side of the room, and two statues representing Comedy and Tragedy either side of the plain, perfectly proportioned, proscenium. All this, or an indication of it, remains. The floorboards have been removed, cleaned and replaced on the range of 'dwarf' brick walls, patterned with mini-arches, thought to have been made by apprentice builders in the original construction, and running at right angles from the stage to the back of the room. Macqueen-Pope installed a bar underneath the surviving balcony and widened the gangways; the audience, or a great part of it, was in perpetual motion during a variety bill.

The theatre re-opened, finally, for Christmas in 1922 with *Cinderella*. Macqueen-Pope moved on – to the Duke of York's – in 1924 and the lease was taken by the comedian and producer Archie Pitt, Gracie Fields' first husband, who used the stage for rehearsals and previews prior to his West End openings. One of Fields' biggest hits, *Walk This Way*, her last revue for Pitt before they divorced, was previewed here en route to a Christmas 1931 season at the Winter Garden (on the site of today's New London Theatre). When Pitt's lease expired in 1934, the theatre was commandeered by amateurs and local schoolchildren. In 1936, the BBC leased the entire East Court wing of the palace and, while broadcasting the world's first regular high-definition public television from the new studios, used the theatre as a storeroom until 1982. The fire of 1980, which burned a large part of the building to the ground, stopped short of the theatre when the wind suddenly changed direction, but the dressing rooms at the back of the stage were badly damaged and subsequently demolished. The Willis organ escaped lightly, too, as many of the pipes happened to have been removed for maintenance at the time; it still stands, and is in use, in need of major restoration at some stage in the fundraising future.

Once again, the Ally Pally, as it is affectionately known, arose from the rubble and the cinders in a major restoration and re-opened in 1988. The 'historic interest' recognition came with the Grade II listing in 1996. The green light for the East Court restoration programme came through in 2015, £18.8 million from Heritage Lottery Funding, £6.8 million from Haringey Council, with a further £1 million to be raised in private donations. Approximately £8 million of that total sum is designated for the theatre, which will have new retractable seating allowing for end-stage productions – when the seating will rise on the slightly raked floor and continue in a block through the circle – as well as a choice of staging configurations in the hall itself. The circle, which has a far more dramatic sweep than it would appear when viewed from the stage, will be fully reseated when the end-stage option is not in operation.

The stage may serve as a performance area: it is large, roomy, and very high, the remnants of a stage curtain hanging evocatively from the flies and, to stage left, there is a wooden cabinet holding the ceramic cylinders once used for dimming the lights. The surfaces, plasterwork and semi-rendered salmon-pink peeling walls are to be left, as far as possible, exactly as they are, so that the magic of the space, as at Wilton's Music Hall, or in the other significant, very different, remaining variety house in London, Hoxton Hall, will leave its stamp on audiences and performances alike down the ages, a theatre that, Janus-like, looks two ways, backwards and forwards, at once.

Alexandra Palace Theatre
Alexandra Palace Way, London N22 7AY
www.alexandrapalace.com

*An old stage curtain hangs from the flies. A wooden cabinet to the left held ceramic cylinders for dimming the lights.*

# BBC Radio Theatre

BBC buffs, comedy fans and free-ticket wallahs know all about the BBC Radio Theatre. You can choose a show online and turn up on the night with a printed ticket with a barcode, like an airline boarding pass – as indeed you can at the Royal Opera nowadays, too. It nestles comfortably in the conjoined nexus of the old 1932 Broadcasting House in Langham Place and the spectacular 2007 architectural development, which now sits like a brilliant horseshoe compromise between the Art Deco original and the outer office-dominated limits of Great Portland Street.

This venue was known as the BBC Concert Hall – renamed the Radio Theatre in 1994 – and the current version combines original Art Deco elements with modern comfort, a seating capacity of 300 and a renewed sense of purpose at the heart of the BBC. Approaching the theatre, you enter an oblong bar with views on one side of the spectacularly relocated BBC newsroom, the hub of the whole organisation; on the other side, beyond the extended café area, there are large windows giving on to the grey stone grandeur of Portland Place – once renowned as the finest street in eighteenth-century London – with its non-stop activity of taxis and tourists wandering between Oxford Circus and Regent's Park.

Arriving at the BBC these days is quite different from how it used to be. For a start, you are made to feel welcome. The £1 billion renovation has opened the whole place up without, amazingly, destroying its special calibre: there's a new piazza with coffee shops and outdoor access to watching concerts and the flagship daily news TV feature *The One Show* in operation, and an overall sense of the public joining in. This atmosphere is epitomised by the Radio Theatre, designed

*As viewed from the stage, the new red flip-up seats are surrounded by 1932 Art Deco friezes, light fittings and BBC clock.*

*Architect Val Meyer called Broadcasting House a 'top hat' design because of its cylindrical suavity in Portland stone.*

*The public can access free tickets for quiz and comedy shows.*

by Val Meyer as part of his 1932 remit in Portland stone. The whole building was a Modernist undertaking, still resembling a grounded ocean-going liner – Meyer called it a 'top hat' design, because of its cylindrical suavity. It rises magnificently above the surrounding area, decorated with brilliant and controversial Eric Gill stone friezes; Prospero and Ariel, spirits of tempest and wind-blown mischief, guard the former main entrance. This atmosphere of stylish innovation carries over into Meyer's theatre, just about.

There are red plush tip-up seats. The low-level classical friezes remain. The proportions of the arena are the same as they were in 1932 (when ticket prices ranged from two shillings to seven-and-sixpence, i.e. 10p to 38p). The 36-foot-wide stage end fans subtly out to a 46-foot width at the back of the auditorium, which is 106 feet long, but the Art Deco connection is minimal, as it is in other refurbished or redecorated Art Deco theatres like the Whitehall (now the neutrally transformed Trafalgar Studios) or the Fortune in Great Russell Street opposite Drury Lane. Still, the simple, stylish Art Deco clock remains at the front of the balcony, surviving the major technical overhaul in 2007, when the corporation was gearing up to its new challenges on all sides, political and creative. The original floor-level bas-reliefs by Gilbert Bayes on each side of the auditorium are intact, and very beautiful, in their invocation of classic scenes of dancing, ball games, sacrifice and lascivious lolling. Above them, at knee-level, is a panoply of Art Deco light fittings, which change in colour from a modest mauve

pre-set to a warm yellow as the show begins. Somewhere in the house is the original 1932 Compton organ, but the walls are covered – very astutely – with a sort of compromise plaster in a grey finish.

The original BBC Concert Hall was one of just twenty-two recording studios in the 'liner' and a small masterpiece of Art Deco detail and design. The feeling you get when sitting in the audience is extraordinary. The BBC is the greatest, and biggest, employer of creative talent in the United Kingdom; audiences for talk and quiz shows in the Radio Theatre are made to feel part of a process, and an ideology, that echoes in the very heart of our democracy and notion of free speech. That is why seeing the simplest of comedy shows or the tritest of quiz programmes in this space has such a special feel about it. A voice might be heard, something might change. And all of that is enhanced by the tradition, and the architecture, of the building.

BBC Radio Theatre

Broadcasting House, Portland Place, London W1A 1AA

www.bbc.co.uk

# Charing Cross Theatre

The Charing Cross Theatre, along with the Arts Theatre in Great Newport Street, is the smallest commercial producing theatre in London. While the Arts has stayed exactly where it is since 1927, the Charing Cross, which dates back to the same year, is the latest version of the famous Players' Theatre, home of Victorian burlesque and pantomime, the 'Late Joys' music hall and progenitor of Sandy Wilson's 1920s pastiche musical comedy *The Boy Friend* (1953), one of the longest-running British musicals before the advent of rock and electrified bands, still performed all over the world.

The current venue in a small arcaded passageway off Villiers Street, the short, steep thoroughfare linking the Strand to the Embankment, dates from 1990, several yards further along from the original Players', which opened for business in two of the Hungerford Arches under Charing Cross station in 1946; it replicates that original in its long, tunnel-like auditorium with raked seating and a bar at the rear. It's a simple, stark, utilitarian interior, with grey decorative arches on the side-walls, a colour scheme of grey and red, functional electric torches on the long boxed galleries on either side of the stage and in the foyer. This followed a refurbishment in 2005, when the name was altered, under new management, to the New Players' Theatre; it was altered yet again to the Charing Cross Theatre in 2011, and the Players' Bar and Kitchen was revamped. This process of rehousing and modernisation was prompted by a major office block development in the immediate vicinity.

The story of the Charing Cross Theatre is rooted in the convergence of two strands of activity: those of the Players' company launched in Soho in 1927, and of Victorian music hall under the arches dating from 1864. Hungerford market had

*The Charing Cross Theatre replicates some features, and dimensions, of the renowned Players' in Villiers Street, with topographical roots in Victorian music hall.*

been demolished to make way for Charing Cross station in 1863. Carlo Gatti, a Swiss-Italian immigrant, who had owned a restaurant serving coffee and ice-cream in the market, had leased two arches from the South Eastern Railway and secured a music hall licence in 1867; he opened two large rooms, one for billiards with seventeen tables, the other a coffee room with kitchen and offices. With the new licensing, the billiards room was converted into a music hall, the audience seated at tables.

With the installation of a chairman to supervise the 'turns', this venue became known as Gatti's in the Arches – Carlo died in 1878 and his widow and daughter, followed by his grandchildren, took over the business – and was the model for the participatory nature of the Players' music hall nights. The venue was renamed Gatti's Hungerford Palace

of Varieties in 1883; refurbished and given a small gallery in 1886; and much sketched, and then painted, by Walter Sickert in 1888, several years before he produced his more famous studies of the Bedford Music Hall in Camden Town. Sickert's *Gatti's Hungerford Palace of Varieties: Second Turn of Miss Katie Lawrence* was one of the most controversial paintings of the late nineteenth century. The waif-like figure of the young singer in a loose-fitting yellow dress was curiously daring and ambiguous, while the indefinite quality of Sickert's lady in the stalls wearing a large red hat suggested that she was almost certainly a prostitute. Gatti's, which had a robust music hall reputation for being both disreputable and popular, closed down in 1903, and the arches housed a cinema between 1910 and 1923, then hosted boxing tournaments. After another period of closure, a

*The simple, functional backstage area dates from a 2005 refurbishment.*

*Electric torches decorate the theatre as well as the foyer, one of them placed next to a bell to summon the audience to the play.*

fleapit cinema known as the Forum, showing mostly foreign and salacious movies, opened in 1928, before being claimed by the government in wartime as an auxiliary fire service depot and storeroom.

The Players', first known briefly as Playroom Six, opened in 1927 in a tiny New Compton Street theatre (with 100 seats) and marked the auspicious London debut of Peggy Ashcroft whom, coincidentally, Sickert painted often, in a play called *One Day More* (not to be confused with the rousing Act One finale of that title in *Les Misérables*), adapted by Joseph Conrad from his own short story. In 1934, the Players' moved to 43 King Street in Covent Garden, a magnificent town mansion (recently restored), one time home of Lord Russell, First Lord of the Admiralty and, between 1891 and 1929, headquarters of the National Sporting Club and the burgeoning sport of professional boxing. Throughout the middle years of the nineteenth century this address had been converted into an hotel featuring Evans Music-and-Supper Rooms; the Players' Theatre Club operated on the third floor only, soon closed, but re-opened in 1936 as the New Players', producing Victorian cabaret, the germ of the Late Joys, so called in a reference to a man called Joy, Evans' predecessor. Evans' rooms were therefore known colloquially as Evans Late Joys. The Late Joys were indeed late, performances at 11.30 p.m. (and on Tuesdays and Fridays at 1.30 a.m.) following plays given earlier in the evening.

In 1940, the Players' (dropping the 'New' once again) moved, during the Blitz, to the safer below-ground premises of a former nightclub, El Morocco, in Albemarle Street in St James's. The company was now under the sole direction of Leonard Sachs, an actor who became a household name on television between 1953 and 1983, chairing *The Good Old Days*, a music hall programme modelled on the Players' and filmed in the City Varieties in Leeds. Sachs was a co-founder of the New Players' in King Street and gave early opportunities to such future stars as Ian Carmichael, Hattie

Jacques, Maggie Smith and Peter Ustinov. While he served in the war for five years, the company was run by the actress Jean Anderson, and never closed.

On his return, Sachs discovered the abandoned arches in Villiers Street, took out a lease in 1946 and re-opened the new Players' Theatre and their Late Joys. The Players' was always a members' club, but towards the ends of its life in Villiers Street, where a bar situated along the side of the stalls was a distinctive, and often pleasurably distracting, feature, tickets were made available to the general public. The charm of the place persisted, peddling an almost eccentric devotion to the old-style music hall of Gatti's and, every Christmas, producing a Victorian burlesque pantomime, usually one written by J.R. Planché, replete with rhyming couplets, operatic arias and cumbersome puns. The Players' moved to the new Villiers Street premises in 1990, but became homeless in 2002. The theatre has struggled to reinvent itself but, since 2011, under new ownership, there have been attempts to re-establish the Charing Cross as a going concern for new plays and musicals, as well as for musical theatre curios and revivals.

Charing Cross Theatre

The Arches, Villiers Street, London WC2N 6NL

www.charingcrosstheatre.co.uk

*The set for Tennessee Willliams' In the Bar of a Tokyo Hotel, designed by Nicolai Hart-Hansen, complements the sleek lines of the theatre with an opulent sweep.*

EASTWARD HO!

# Wilton's Music Hall

Wilton's Music Hall, the last of the first music halls of the 1850s, was virtually dead and gone itself until the shift in public awareness and opinion about the value and irreplaceable charms and virtues of our old theatres about twenty years ago. The salvation of these embattled premises in the heart of the East End of London is the most spectacular and unexpected act of rescue in recent years. You only have to step inside the rectangular auditorium to be immediately enchanted, as if stepping into Narnia, or through the mud-caked thickets of antiquity into a secret garden of mystery and delight. The theatre sits at right angles to (and behind) the front premises of five crumbling Georgian houses in an alleyway directly parallel to Cable Street where, in a famous street battle of 1936, local people repelled the advance of Oswald Mosley and his black shirt fascists.

The hall, very much as it was when it opened in 1859, has a high stage at one end, an apse at the other. The walls have been left in a teasing, ghostly state of distempered disrepair, a single gallery running round three sides, beneath a vaulted ceiling with ornamental fretted ribs. The most striking feature is the array of eleven 'barley sugar' cast-iron pillars which support the balcony, each one of twenty-five regular helical turns, and each one of a different iron base measurement as the floor descends from the back to the front of the hall in a gentle rake. There is no fixed seating – allowing full adaptability for promenade productions, dance competitions, weddings and parties – but a semi-fixed fore-stage, which

PREVIOUS PAGE *Wilton's Music Hall, much as it was in 1859, showing an apse at the far end and a gallery supported by eleven 'barley sugar' cast-iron pillars.*

RIGHT *A plan to demolish Wilton's was opposed by poet John Betjeman in the mid-1960s. It has retained architectural and cultural significance through periods of neglect and endangerment.*

*The entrance hall gives an idea of the terrace of housing across the hall, retaining as much 'heritage dust' as possible.*

brings performances more directly into the audience. There were no performances here between 1888 – when the place became a mission hall – and December 1997, when the Irish actress Fiona Shaw gave a shuddering, awakening 'acted' recitation of T.S. Eliot's *The Waste Land*, 'breeding lilacs out of the dead land, mixing memory and desire, stirring dull roots with spring rain'.

This sense of the past coming alive in the present is peculiarly haunting in Wilton's. The terrace of housing dates originally from the 1690s. People lived and died in these domestic rooms; sailors and merchants drank in The Prince of Denmark pub, as it was once known (later, *c.*1839, it became the Mahogany Bar, on account of its counters and fittings in mahogany, the first London tavern so decorated), in the first of the five front premises, at 17 Wellclose Square. The area was rich in theatrical tradition. There had been eighteenth-century theatres in nearby Ensign Street, Leman Street and in Alie Street, where David Garrick made his

London debut as Richard III in 1741 at Goodman's Fields Theatre on his way to fame and fortune at Drury Lane; Alie Street would figure in more recent theatrical history when the Half Moon Theatre opened in a converted synagogue there in 1972.

When the West Countryman John Wilton, who had managed the Canterbury Arms music hall in Lambeth, bought the pub in 1850 – The Prince of Denmark, or Old Mahogany, was now known as the Albion Saloon – there was already a concert room at the back. He rebuilt both rooms as his first music hall in 1853, while simultaneously acquiring the leases on the adjacent houses in the alley. By 1859 he was ready, with the help of architect Jacob Maggs, to build his grand music hall across the gardens on the site. A sun-burner chandelier of 300 gas jets and 27,000 cut crystals lit up the mirrored hall, and the audiences flocked. The opening bill included a soprano singing an aria by Thomas Arne, composer of the National Anthem, and an Irish

*The main front doors on Graces Alley in the heart of the East End.*

comedian, Sam Collins, who was the proprietor of Collins' Music Hall (built in 1863, destroyed in 1958) on Islington Green. The most famous 'turn' was George Leybourne, whose signature song, 'Champagne Charlie', was tied in with an obligation by contract with Moët to drink nothing but their champagne in public; the poor man died of liver disease aged forty-two, penniless but full of bubbles.

The place was seriously damaged by fire in 1877 but rebuilt with the raked floor and new proscenium to its current measurements of 55 feet long, 40 feet wide, 40 feet high. However, these works took eight years to finish, by which time Wilton had sold on his hall in 1868 to go and manage the refreshments at the Lyceum Theatre, and the new proprietor, Bill Holland, went bankrupt. The music hall

closed in 1881, and the next seven years are an undisclosed mystery. From 1888 to 1956, Wilton's was a Methodist mission hall, refuge for families of striking dockers in 1889 – this momentous industrial action was at the root of the dockers' subsequent union stronghold in the East End – and a soup kitchen during both world wars. In 1957, the houses were occupied by a rag-sorting depot and warehouse before being acquired by the Greater London Council in 1966 with a view to demolition and development. While streets and other surrounding historic buildings were flattened, a campaign led by theatre historian John Earl and poet John Betjeman saved Wilton's and secured a Grade II listing. Ownership transferred to a trust. Still, nothing much happened for twenty-five years, beyond some dilatory

*Wooden pews at the back of the hall, the walls in a state of distempered disrepair.*

fundraising, a few crucial repairs, some money-making film shoots and a proliferation of plans and false starts.

After *The Waste Land*, Broomhill Opera secured a tenancy for three years from 1999 and renewed public interest in the space. But still it lay empty for another two years until the concert producer Frances Mayhew, who had worked with Broomhill, approached the trust with yet another plan to save it. This involved touting for more business with film and photographic companies and putting in a new bar. Mayhew, who led the campaign for twelve years, was a descendant of the social historian and journalist Henry Mayhew, whose book of ground-level reportage, *London Labour and the London Poor* (1861), highlighted the problems in the docks – over-employment and low pay in a desperately over-crowded labour market – that led to the 1889 strike, so her involvement was both apt and deeply felt. Her task was daunting. Over 40 per cent of the site was precarious and fragile, crumbling faster than she could repair it. With the same architect, Tim Ronalds, who had recently restored the Hackney Empire, she formed a plan of action, a £4 million project in two phases to first restore the hall itself and then to stabilise the houses. In a campaign spearheaded by actor David Suchet alongside Mayhew, £1 million was raised through trust funds and donations, and the first part of the renewal began in the hall: the roof was insulated, the building waterproofed, new heating and air-handling systems installed, and the electrics, sound and lighting upgraded. Meanwhile, the money needed to complete the job was supplied, at last, by a formerly rejected Heritage Lottery bid: £1.8 million, to add to a further £1 million in loans and donations, meant that Phase 2 could begin in 2014. A similar restoration for the houses at the front ensued, with modern skylights placed above Victorian ones, various spaces opened up for usage, a new studio area created above the Mahogany Bar, and Wilton's back stairs rebuilt.

Original features, such as the railway sleepers used as beams on the main central staircase, were retained. The whole idea was only to do the absolutely necessary – renewing lintels, restoring brickwork – and retain as much 'heritage dust' as possible; so, you see two broken Victorian windows in the cosy cocktail bar on the first floor and, nearby, an ancient little birds' nest. Other 'outside' windows are now inside, creating an illusion of further space in a labyrinth of brickwork and benches, stairways, small rooms and port holes. Wilton had merely knocked through walls when he needed to make changes to the theatre; there was a sort of wedge-shaped void between the back wall of the houses and the side wall of the main hall, and this chasm of crumbling brick and dereliction needed the most, and most careful, attention. The furthest of the five houses, 17 Wellclose Square, had been knocked down and rebuilt in the 1980s. This was now incorporated as an ancillary to the new Wilton's, with dressing rooms on top, and kitchen and storage space adjacent to the main bar on ground level.

As well as no permanent seating, the theatre has no wing space, no back stage area and no flying capability. And yet, in the right hands, it's a magic space, and a marvel. And Wilton's is renewed as both a cultural destination in the capital and an educational and recreational resource to the community on its own doorstep. The first line of the dedication on the foundation stone preserved in the foyer, laid in December 1858, is carved on a wooden beam you see as you enter through the main doors of Graces Alley, a stripped back wooden portal with a stone arch and carved pillars: 'To Great Apollo God of Early Morn'. The theatre returns with the sunrise.

Wilton's Music Hall
1 Graces Alley, London E1 8JB
www.wiltons.org.uk

# Barbican Theatre

The Barbican Theatre is part of the Barbican Centre, a symbol of post-war recovery in the bombed City of London, though we didn't get round to building it until 1971. And we didn't get round to opening it – after countless rows and delays in the building schedule – until 1982. The London Symphony Orchestra conducted by Vladimir Ashkenazy opened the concert hall; the cinema flung – or at least pushed – open its doors; and the Royal Shakespeare Company christened its exciting new 'European' auditorium – no centre aisle, electro-magnetically operated individual doors for each row, three narrow circles of only two rows each jutting forwards to the stage – with Shakespeare's *Henry IV, Parts One and Two*, Joss Ackland playing Falstaff. The theatre dazzles even when the safety curtain is in: 50 tons of sparkling stainless steel in corrugated patches which splits and divides horizontally.

The Barbican was the City of London's big civic and cultural statement, comparable perhaps to the Pompidou Centre in Paris or the Lincoln Center in New York. But it is unique in being part of such a major residential complex, with the LSO and the RSC invited to contribute to the planning of the two main halls in the mid-1960s as the construction of the mighty concrete bastion – 300-foot towers and eighteen other forty-three-storey blocks housing over 2,000 apartments – began. A library and an art gallery were included in the arts centre by the architects Chamberlin, Powell and Bon.

The area had already been rich in history and disaster before the maze of streets and warehouses covering 40 acres was flattened by the Luftwaffe on one night of bombing in December 1940. The Barbican includes many remains and reminders of the walls of the Roman fortress site. The un-bombed eleventh-century church of St Giles, patron saint of cripples, is clearly

*The auditorium with the safety curtain down.*

*From these stairs, electro-magnetically operated doors lead to individual rows of the auditorium.*

visible across the water feature running alongside the Barbican's café. This part of the East End was a haven for Jewish émigrés and actors (as well as Shakespeare and Ben Jonson). Grub Street, said Samuel Johnson, was 'much inhabited by writers of small histories, dictionaries and temporary poems'. So an arts centre is both a memorial and a continuation within a scheme designed to recreate a vanished community: the Barbican is home to 4,000 people, 50 per cent of the City of London's residential population, harboured around its echoing walkways, along its wind-swept tunnels and up its forbidding towers, a concrete metropolis with parking for all and a yellow line to help you follow the signs to wherever you think you are going, which is not always where you end up.

The element of confusion in the overpowering brutalist design was deliberate, part of the idea that this was a self-contained city within a city to which it now bore little topographical relationship. And this certainly applies to the arts centre, where no amount of signage is any help to ascertain on what level you are standing. The ground level always seems to be Level 3, or Level 5. The art gallery was supposed to be the main entrance, but nobody uses it, and the nearby sculpture court has no sculpture. Spaces intended for shops are occupied by offices. Outside, there are distinct 'fortressy' attributes of a semi-circular motif, spiral vaulting, lozenge-shaped apertures, crenellated edges and arrow slits that find their more controlled way inside the foyers and auditoria. The concrete inside the centre – all the concrete was cast in situ – has a laboriously hand-drilled texture, like the surface of a frozen, spiky meringue.

The theatre is the second in London – after the Criterion – to exist entirely underground, on five subterranean storeys. The stage is 60 feet wide, the grid 110 feet above the stage. Lorries with scenery drive in and drop down on a long platform to the fourth (stage) lower level. All this was arranged to specifications of Peter Hall and the designer John Bury of the RSC. The deal was their guaranteed tenure, with offices and rehearsal space, for a peppercorn rent. The RSC's first London home, in 1960, was the Aldwych Theatre, and the move to the city was supposed to have happened in 1970. By the time they moved in, Trevor Nunn had succeeded Hall by fifteen years. His designer for *Henry IV*, John Napier, immediately exploited the epic potential of the stage with a set of four platforms carrying different

structures and linked in various permutations, and their first Christmas show, *Peter Pan* (casting a male actor as Peter for the first time) was a fantastical extravaganza with grassy knolls, lagoons and a magnificently built *Jolly Roger* in Neverland.

Nunn had wanted dark wooden cladding inside the auditorium, so the intended pale yew was ditched in favour of Peruvian walnut. The RSC had also insisted on a 120-foot extruding concrete fly tower to store scenery in a quick-changing repertory system, and the architects had disguised it by creating the second largest conservatory in London (the largest is at Kew Gardens), a paradisiacal, light-filled retreat of greenery, exotic plants, cacti, water and terrapins that has been, from day one, a popular party destination and function room for hire as well as internal use. But the RSC, now operating three theatres in Stratford-upon-Avon and two in London (the Barbican has an unlovely bunker-

*The stage in the course of being changed, three narrow circles in the auditorium jutting towards the action.*

like Pit for experimental work and new plays), was in dire financial straits. The 1984 Priestley report came to their aid, concluding that the RSC was massively under-funded and recommending Arts Council funding parity with the National Theatre. The Nunn and Terry Hands RSC of the 1980s gave the Barbican Antony Sher's Richard III, Michael Gambon's King Lear, Juliet Stevenson's Rosalind and Derek Jacobi's Cyrano de Bergerac, great performances all. But when Adrian Noble succeeded Hands as artistic director in 1991, he became restless, and – in stark contrast to the audiences who thronged the place – dissatisfied with the theatre.

By 1997 Noble had reduced the RSC's presence in the building to six months a year and there was increasing difficulty over internal relationships and delays in meeting scheduling deadlines. In the following year, the Barbican's third managing director, John Tusa (the former BBC journalist had succeeded Henry Wrong and Detta O'Cathain) launched Bite – Barbican International Theatre Events – and, as the RSC slunk away for good in 2002, Bite was established as a year-round festival, the best thing that has happened in the venue apart, perhaps, from the 2001 acoustic and aesthetic refurbishment in the concert hall and the new Dutch flying system recently installed in the theatre, with a state-of-the-art computerised control centre in the grid that resembles a crazed villain's lair in the last reel of a James Bond movie.

The arts centre part of the Barbican build had cost a staggering £156 million and, between 2003 and 2006, while the centre remained in operation, there was a £14 million project to improve toilets and lighting, to lower the new 85-foot-long bar in the lower foyer (level unknown) and to extend a steel and glass bridge right across the main foyer area with access to Silk Street on one side and the external

*The fly system control interface.*

*The new £3.4 million fly floor, a sci-fi lair of unequalled sophistication in London, designed in Holland.*

plaza on the other. Silk Street – where some cheap-looking golden statuettes, stuck on the awning by Detta O'Cathain, were summarily despatched by John Tusa – was finally established as the main entrance, though you can still tippy-toe along the yellow lines from other points around the complex. The stage door is immediately to your left as you face this glass door frontage, with a spacious ramped corridor leading you to the front reception and information desk. No London theatre has a great restaurant, and the Barbican is no exception.

But the theatre and concert hall remain at the head of the field in range of programming and quality of delivery. Bite has established the Barbican as our main outlet for visiting foreign and native work from modern maestri like Peter Brook, Robert Lepage, Robert Wilson, Peter Stein, Ivo van Hove and Michael Clark; and companies like the Schaubühne in Berlin, the Théâtre de la Ville in Paris, the

Sydney Theatre Company and our own Complicite and Cheek by Jowl extend and elaborate the theatrical language every year. Even the RSC under its new artistic director, Gregory Doran, has undergone a change of heart, and the disastrously low profile of the company in London since the exodus in 2002 is slowly being buffed up again with limited-season visits to the stage they were gifted by the City in the first place.

Barbican Theatre
Silk Street, London EC2Y 8DS
www.barbican.org.uk

# Hackney Empire

An alternative comedian, said our last great music hall and variety star, Sir Ken Dodd, is a comedian who isn't funny. The alternative comedians of the 1980s, funny or not, were deadly serious in joining the campaign to save Frank Matcham's magnificent variety palace, the last surviving example of the architect's several variety houses in Greater London. 'New Variety' featured the likes of Griff Rhys Jones, Ben Elton, Dawn French, Jennifer Saunders and Lenny Henry treading the same boards as Charlie Chaplin, W.C. Fields, Stan Laurel, Marie Lloyd and Harry Houdini. Two of the original stone steps up to the stage door are preserved by the new stage door, and the original entrances to the upper circle and gallery on the side elevation are still used by the public today.

The fringe impresario Roland Muldoon was the spearhead for the Empire's salvation, forming a preservation trust after the place had been used as a bingo hall for twenty years, launching his campaign with just £8,000 in the kitty and re-opening as a theatrical venue in 1986, on the Empire's eighty-fifth anniversary. It cannot be over-stated how close we came to losing this wonderful theatre. As if to emphasise the point, when the theatre re-opened for a second time in 2004, after a three-year, £22 million refurbishment and rebuild, the lyrics of Marie Lloyd's most famous song, 'The Boy I Love is Up in the Gallery' were painted onto an open plaster book above the proscenium, and the numbers used to identify the music hall acts, as in the hymn numbers on a church column in the nave, posted either side of it; that number '04' signifies both an item on the bill and the date of re-opening.

The first all-electric theatre in the capital was built in 1901 for Oswald Stoll in just thirty-eight weeks at a cost of £40,000.

*The architect Frank Matcham's unerring eye for scale and proportion is seen in the relationship between the stage and three-tiered auditorium.*

*Ornamentation either side of the stage contains a variety bill number – 04 – the year of a major refurbishment.*

Matcham had to modify his plans as he went along, for Stoll changed his mind about housing his company headquarters in the Empire and commissioned Matcham to build an even grander variety theatre, the Coliseum, in St Martin's Lane, in order to compete with the Hippodrome (which Matcham also designed) on his immediate West End doorstep. So there's a more muted grandeur about the Empire, but still a grandeur, with its terra cotta façade of arches, bays and pediment, short towers and Byzantine domes, and the stone figure of Euterpe, Greek muse of lyric poetry and music, on top.

An abundance of stained glass in the theatre starts on the elegant canopy to the frontage, leading into a fine vestibule with a double staircase, finished in marble (and covered in linoleum during the bingo years). Half-way up, going into the circle, there's a pink marble seat allegedly donated by the Shah of Persia to Queen Victoria, but it seems too inseparable from the building for this to be true. The opulent flourish of this foyer is contained in the rectangular formality of its ceiling. The plasterwork, as throughout the auditorium, is carefully composed, not overly ornate, with three large roundels, deliberately restored, then re-faded in the refurbishment, of Handel, Haydn and Mozart on the left-hand side facing a plaque opposite for the entrepreneur Alan Sugar's parents, who ran a fish and chip shop over the road; Sugar was a key donor in the campaign to save the Empire.

Inside, there's an atmosphere full of Eastern promise in the three-tiered auditorium, and of fading Byzantine glamour in the great sweep of the place, the muted red colouring, the elephants on the proscenium domes, the pastel frescoes, the sculpted angels ('angels' in the modern theatre are the financial backers of productions) and rococo paintings around the proscenium, the elegant arches and pilasters guarding the two cantilevered, beautifully fronted circles. From the stage, where there is a unique 'bastard' prompt in the stage right corner (the prompt corner is usually at stage left), you can see every seat in the house – this is a two-way process, a feature of Matcham's unerring eye for scale and accuracy in his design technique – and when the stage rake was flattened at some expense, more easily to accommodate dance and opera companies, so was the rake in the auditorium adjusted, preserving a harmonious relationship between stage and stalls. The balcony alone seats 300 people in an overall capacity of 1,000, but it is alarmingly steep, fitted with long, curving, uninterrupted velveteen-covered benches, and is thus deemed a health and safety liability where children are concerned; so it is closed down, ironically enough, for the theatre's packed-out pantomime seasons, which have run since 1988 and kept the whole operation just about afloat.

The ornamental ceiling of the auditorium is satisfyingly complex, and every surface of the theatre is replete with remarkable detail, some of it accidental. The ten boxes around the back of the dress circle were originally decorated in a pretty red flock wallpaper 'by royal appointment to Buckingham Palace, the White House and the Hackney Empire', which was nonetheless hung upside down; a new version of the same wallpaper was ordered for the refurbishment and hung upside down again in strict observance of the original misdemeanour. The building is littered with fine old Victorian radiators, which all still

*The rectangular formality of the foyer ceiling reflects the opulent flourish of the theatre.*

work. The location of the bar at the back of the stalls, with its agreeably wide concourse, is a legacy of the variety hall; patrons would linger there, supping, until a particular act tickled their collective fancy and they would rush down into their seats, hence the time-honoured phrase, 'bring down the house'. Some small wooden tables 'up' there have been retained from the bingo period.

One of the last bills of the old variety days, in 1956, proclaims Tod Slaughter and his company in *Maria Marten, or The Murder in the Red Barn* and G.H. Elliott, 'The Chocolate-Coloured Coon', who appeared in blackface and white suit singing 'I Used to Sigh for the Silvery Moon' and 'Lily of Laguna'. In the same year, the Empire was bought by ATV as a studio for such popular television programmes as *Take Your Pick* (with Michael Miles) and *Oh Boy!*, the pioneering rock 'n' roll show produced by Jack Good, both broadcast live. Mecca took over the venue as a bingo hall in 1965 and did nothing too injurious to the

structure or decoration, painting over or boarding over as they saw fit. Twenty years later, Muldoon moved in to fight off a demolition threat, and in 1995 Ralph Fiennes played a memorable Hamlet. The major refurbishment and partial rebuild on one side added an extended orchestra pit, a fly tower, a new studio theatre, improved dressing rooms and education and hospitality facilities.

In 2013, the theatre won a ten-year battle with an insurance firm over construction costs incurred in the refurbishment when the building's contractor went into administration, leaving £1.1 million worth of work incomplete. Alan Sugar came to the rescue for a second time, and the award was used to repay his further loan. The theatre made up that 'loss' by selling off an out-building for the development of luxury flats and a small row of mews houses to the left of the stage door, while retaining a very useful rehearsal and studio space in the ground level of the apartment development, immediately opposite the stage door. The old Marie Lloyd pub on the corner disappeared, replaced by a different sort of 'club' bar, which serves up drink, food and new music.

The Empire is less financially and socially secure than you would expect in the diverse and lively East End borough, old stomping ground of playwright Harold Pinter (who is memorialised in a hospitality room). The Arts Council support is unexceptional, and the local council almost totally unsupportive. However, it seems a momentous, iconic destination in this area, described in a *Times* newspaper survey of 2011 as 'the creative heart of London', with more artists – in fashion, food, art and music – in residence than in any other European quartier. The lively Arcola Theatre is in nearby Dalston, and the Empire sits on Mare Street alongside the London College of Fashion, the new Hackney Picturehouse, a model of an independent cinema with a bar/kitchen café as good as its five-screen programme, and Hackney Town Hall, which is directly next door, set back from the street behind a public square of palm trees and seating. The Central Library and Museum make up the third side of the square opposite the theatre in a cultural hub without equal in the capital beyond the South Bank.

Hackney Empire

291 Mare Street, London E8 1EJ

www.hackneyempire.co.uk

*Domes, frescoes, arches and plasterwork convey an air of fading Byzantine glamour.*

# Theatre Royal Stratford East

Several years before she finally threw in the towel in 1979 and retired to France, the director Joan Littlewood posed for a photograph on a pile of rubble outside the Theatre Royal, Stratford East. She was still hoping to launch a Fun Palace and had staged a series of improvisatory events on this wasteland. The plain but imposing façade of the Victorian theatre where she produced a series of world-famous productions between 1958 (*A Taste of Honey*) and 1963 (*Oh, What a Lovely War!*) is a backdrop to her irrepressible cheek and belief in the value of popular entertainment in a deprived community. Littlewood, hailed by Peter Brook as 'the most galvanising director in mid-twentieth-century Britain', died in 2002, but that photograph is mummified in the bronze statue by Philip Jackson now standing a few feet from the theatre.

Littlewood is wearing the same costermonger's cap and London Borough of Newham dustman's jacket she borrowed for the shoot; a black plaque on the façade commemorates 'the founder of modern young people's theatre', and that spirit still informs the work at Stratford, where the audience is the liveliest and most ethnically diverse in Britain, let alone London. Littlewood settled in the run-down theatre with her Theatre Workshop company in 1953 after fifteen years' hard slog in Cumbria, Manchester, on tour and around Europe, developing not just original plays – many of the early ones written by the folk singer and political activist Ewan MacColl, whom she married – but also items from the European repertoire in her own version of a commedia dell'arte free-wheeling, internationally minded socialist company.

The Theatre Royal sits now on the fringe of the Olympic Park and a regenerated area of the East End of London subsequent

*The beautiful ceiling in a perfect 1884 auditorium, with Donald Albery's chandelier, has overlooked Joan Littlewood's modern classics and raucous pantomime.*

*Onstage, a set design by Ellen Cairns for Americanised Chekhov fits snugly into the horseshoe, seen from the dress circle.*

to the Olympic Games of 2012. In its immediate vicinity it remains a beacon of vivacity and optimism in what is glumly designated a 'theatre quarter' – there's a shiny new arts centre, Stratford Circus, immediately next door (since 2001) and, where rubble once piled high after the area was razed to the ground in the late 1960s, there's a busy segment of the University of East London and a Stratford Picturehouse cinema built over a large Pizza Express. It all makes for an undistinguished agglomeration of four-square glass and concrete design; even the Theatre Royal has joined in, adding two utilitarian glass flanks of rehearsal rooms, offices and social spaces in an extensive eighteen-month rebuild and refurbishment at the dawn of the millennium.

The theatre's brick façade, now painted red but once grey and later blue, with a projecting bay window, was in fact the wall of a wheelwrights' warehouse. It opened for theatrical business in 1884 with a play about Cardinal Richelieu by Bulwer Lytton. It is odd that the reputation it soon acquired for melodrama, variety and rare classics prefigured almost exactly Littlewood's Theatre Workshop. The entrance, now as then, is to the right of the building. A need for more space led, in 1891, to the acquisition of a fish shop on Angel Lane, and its garden; the effect was to create a long ramp of a foyer running alongside the auditorium, leading to the bar at the back, which veers off again at right angles. That far exit (an outside entrance back into the long bar) was the front of the fish shop, and the garden, walking back right through to the end of the bar, is now the back half of the stage; the stage's depth went from 18 feet deep to its present 38 feet, one of the deepest in London.

Frank Matcham effected some minor decorative alterations in 1902. His work on the sloping foyer is remarkable: a hall of mirrors of various sizes, their lower frames following the slope, their upper ones decorated with royal insignia, some squashed, some brazen, to fit the

*Cartoons by Terence 'Larry' Parkes decorating a backstage staircase.*

*The fly floor and grid, ropes at the ready.*

wall space and match the other plaster ornamentation on the red-painted walls. The informality, and redness, carries through to the jewel of an intimate auditorium, with two balconies supported on cast-iron columns. The plaster ornamentation is fine but simple, not luxuriant. There was a backstage fire in 1921 and twice-nightly variety and revue restored in 1927. But the theatre, which had been owned by the Fredericks family for nearly fifty years, closed in 1933, opened again with a succession of different managers, closed again in wartime, then resumed business under new ownership in 1946. On 16 January 1950, the Theatre Royal transmitted the first play televised 'live' from a theatre, *Spring-Heeled Jack*, starring Tod Slaughter (a 'thud and blunder' merchant of the old touring theatre school) as the diabolical villain of Victorian melodrama.

When Littlewood and her general manager, and lover, Gerry Raffles dropped anchor in 1953, actors mended the seats, unblocked the drains, put out buckets to catch the rain and even dossed down (illegally) in the rude dressing rooms. The theatre was tucked away behind Stratford Broadway – with its grandiose Victorian monuments of St John's Anglican Church, the Old Town Hall and an obelisk-like drinking fountain in memory of banker and philanthropist Samuel Gurney – among rows of small terraced houses. Angel Lane ran alongside, still busy in 1953, still bustling in the 1960s; the actors were regular customers of Bert and May Scagnelli in the Café L'Ange, feasting, when they could afford to, on home-cured ham and great wedges of apple-pie.

Theatre Workshop's first big successes were Brecht's *The Good Soldier Schweyk* in 1955 and Brendan Behan's *The Quare Fellow* in the following year, opening sixteen days after John Osborne's *Look Back in Anger* at the Royal Court and thought by many, in its riotous language and debate about capital punishment, to be just as significant and influential. The composer Lionel Bart's *Oliver!* (1960) was a West End phenomenon, but his creative soul was with Littlewood; *Oliver!* was preceded at Stratford East by his low-life acidic musical idyll *Fings Ain't Wot They Used T'Be* (1959), described by Littlewood as '*Guys and Dolls* with its flies open'. Littlewood's actors included Barbara Windsor, Toni Palmer, Avis Bunnage, Harry H. Corbett, George A. Cooper, Brian Murphy, Murray Melvin and Richard Harris; and she worked with two of the greatest designers of the last century, John Bury and Sean Kenny.

After *Lovely War*, the theatre faltered and was threatened altogether in the redevelopment plans. The doors were kept open by visiting companies. Littlewood returned with overtly political satire: *MacBird!*, which wittily, and in rhyming couplets, fed on conspiracy theories of Lyndon Johnson as Macbeth in the aftermath of the Kennedy assassination, and *Mrs Wilson's Diary*, based on a *Private Eye* spoof of Harold Wilson's poetically inclined wife, Mary, ruminating on Downing Street shenanigans – while Raffles fought to save the building from the wrecking ball. Littlewood returned again for one last go in 1972, revisiting past hits and bringing on the writer-director who succeeded her, Ken Hill. But Raffles, having saved the theatre and at

Joan Littlewood

last achieved some kind of funding stability, died suddenly, aged fifty-one, in April 1975. A heartbroken Littlewood effectively retired at this point. Subsequent artistic directors have included Clare Venables, Philip Hedley (for twenty-five years) and Kerry Michael, a smart and modest operator seriously plugged into the local community and tactfully mindful of the theatre's great history, who moved on after twelve eventful years in 2017.

There was a minor refurbishment in the early 1990s when some original Matcham stencilled wood panelling was uncovered in the auditorium, the black and gold frieze restored along the upper circle walls, and two floor-level boxes reconstructed, not too convincingly, on either side of the proscenium. The big changes came in 1999 with the glass flanks – which now include an informal Littlewood museum comprising her library, photographs, set models and posters – a new internal spiral staircase from circle to upper circle level, with brass rails, and new carpeting with a fleur-de-lys motif throughout. No more hard benches in the upper gallery: instead, high-backed plush red seats as good as those downstairs, where 'the nobs' are few and far between anyway.

With the glass flanks, the theatre extended backwards, too, even beyond the brick back wall of the fishmongers' garden, to include a comfortable new green room and dressing rooms, corridors lined with production photos and all the Littlewood obituaries. In the foyer, the outer wall on the right-hand side was broken through to the new extension to accommodate a secondary bar area (ices, soft drinks and sweets) and a photographic gallery dedicated to Avis Bunnage and the black lace, jewel-encrusted, figure-hugging dress she wore in her recruitment song in *Lovely War*, promising to 'make a man of any one of you'.

Finally, the ceiling in the auditorium was imaginatively restored around the beautiful chandelier the West End producer Donald Albery gave to Littlewood in 1964. This is one of a pair Albery owned, the other hanging in the Wyndham's, where he transferred all Littlewood's hits. The ceiling centrepiece motifs are the fleur-de-lys, the Tudor rose, and four Versailles sun-bursts amid the decorative panels. It is reassuring to know that only the paupers in the upper gallery can properly see this mini-masterpiece. The work goes on. Kerry Michael opened a new studio space in the café across the small adjacent square named after Gerry Raffles. And a new canopy, with twinkling lights (and not just for the panto season) is taking shape right across the frontage, elaborating on the small 1963 awning above the main entrance.

Theatre Royal Stratford East

Gerry Raffles Square, London E15 1BN

www.stratfordeast.com

WEST END JEWELS

# St Martin's Theatre

The onset of the First World War intervened with the building of the St Martin's, home of *The Mousetrap* since 1974, probably the most distinctively original, surprising and delightful small theatre in the West End. W.G.R. Sprague's inspired concoction in Ionic columns and three storeys, with a stunningly discreet auditorium of polished Italian walnut balconies and balustrades, opened in 1916, three years after its non-identical 'twin', the adjacent Ambassadors. It was a commission by Lord Willoughby de Broke, the 19th Baron, renowned for his interest in hunting and politics, and has remained in the family's ownership ever since, prompting the *Architectural Review* to commend its English Georgian domestic character and 'feel' of a private theatre provided by a patron for his guests.

There is no room here for gold leaf and lavish plasterwork in what is in effect an individual interim statement between the Edwardian last flourish and the Art Deco revolution. Family portraits and landscapes of the family seat at Compton Verney in Warwickshire – now in the hands of a charitable trust operating the place as an art gallery – line the stairways. The coat of arms is enshrined over the proscenium, doing double service for its complementary heraldic emblem above the enscrolled decorative cartouche on the façade that was blown down in the Blitz and not replaced. The de Brokes authorised a complete renovation in 1960, recreating as much of the original design as possible; the lease taken out by Bernard Delfont during the war had now reverted to the family. And there was a further redecoration by theatre designer Carl Toms in 1996, restoring the exceptionally attractive foyer, setting off the wooden interior against red silk wallpaper

*A blue plaque on the theatre's frontage marks* The Mousetrap's *fiftieth-anniversary performance.*

*This clock on the mantelpiece of the set is the oldest prop still in use in the West End.*

and red woven carpets, and introducing a new safety curtain with a jazzy logo. Because of the exceptionally long occupation of one play, over twice as long now than in its theatre of origin next door, which is still thought of as the home of *The Mousetrap*, the theatre is probably the least generally known of all West End houses, and well worth rediscovering.

Not only is the auditorium unique, there are architectural treats and treasures all over the building. There is a beautiful centrepiece with a glass dome in the auditorium ceiling – which is separately protected by National Heritage – and a Hogarth bar at the back of the stalls that has the hushed, exclusive atmosphere of an old-style gentlemen's club, complete with eighteenth-century prints, striped green wallpaper and a permanent display of antique mousetraps, vicious little contraptions baring their teeth and gathering dust under glass casing ribbed with polished wooden strips. More poignantly, the inner foyer displays a plaque with a bas-relief by Eric Gill commemorating the beautiful actress Meggie Albanesi who died aged twenty-four in December 1923 after a rapid descent into alcoholism, promiscuity and a botched abortion following a disastrous love affair with the actor Owen Nares, whose wife had issued an ultimatum along 'her or me' lines after she discovered it. Albanesi appeared here in Clemence Dane's *A Bill of Divorcement*, ironically enough, in 1921, shortly after appearing opposite Nares in John Galsworthy's *The First and Last* in another theatre, directed by Basil Dean. And Dean, smitten with Albanesi himself, commissioned the plaque for the St Martin's where

she had scored such a big success. One critic praised 'her astonishing talent to jump from comedy to tragedy', while the magisterial James Agate proclaimed: 'You felt that she had not only thought out her parts, but fought them out within her own bosom.' She clearly died far too young.

Subsequent notable presentations were Karel Čapek's *R.U.R.* (1923), starring Basil Rathbone and introducing the word 'robot' into the English language, Arnold Ridley's perennial thriller *The Ghost Train* (1925), Mordaunt Sharp's *The Green Bay Tree* (1933), widely acknowledged as the first modern gay play, the 1938 premiere of J.B. Priestley's Yorkshire comedy warhorse *When We Are Married* and the hilarious Joyce Grenfell in cabaret in 1951 and 1954. Anthony Shaffer's innovative thriller *Sleuth* opened in 1970, starring Anthony Quayle and Keith Baxter, and ran for three years until *The Mousetrap* producer Peter Saunders moved his unprecedented hit across from the Ambassadors. Saunders sold the management of *The Mousetrap* and the lease of the St Martin's to Stephen Waley-Cohen's Mousetrap Productions in 1994.

On the stage itself, the design of the play – Roger Furse's original single setting was modified in a more baronial make-over by Anthony Holland in 1965 – is fastidiously maintained and renewed as if the show really were still happening in 1952, but only the clock on the mantelpiece, the longest-running prop in the West End, has survived the entire duration, beating off the challenge of the leather armchair, replaced in 2004 after warming bottoms for a mere half century. The longest-serving member of the cast is Derek

*The wooden and canvas backstage wind machine, the name of* The Mousetrap's *producer visible above the cranking handle.*

Guyler, whose recorded voice on the wireless bulletin has been heard at every performance since opening night in the Ambassadors on 25 November 1952. Myse Monte played Mrs Boyle for thirteen years, and David Raven, Major Metcalf, for eleven. Maisie Wilmer-Brown was wardrobe mistress from opening night for over twenty-one years. An old-fashioned wooden and canvas wind-machine, with a cranking handle that makes it resemble a medieval spit, stands ready in the wings, the name of Peter Saunders incongruously daubed on one side. Two types of stage snow are stored backstage in rudimentary containers, one for the actors to shower on their shoulders like seasonal dandruff as they enter Monkwell Manor during the snow storm, the other to create a blizzard effect behind the window, spilling onto a white polyester dressing of the glass panes.

There has been the odd security leak on exactly whodunnit. Taxi drivers are rumoured to spill the beans if the tip on the fare to the theatre is too mean or non-existent. A whole range of *Mousetrap*-related humorous topics is covered in a permanent display of newspaper cartoons in the dress circle bar – one of Cookson's for the long-defunct *Evening News* shows one tuxedoed wag at an anniversary shindig telling a fellow guest, 'I believe there is another party upstairs for the We-Know-Who-Did-It society.' Agatha Christie decreed that no film of the play could be made until the stage show finished; two entrepreneurs who bought the rights bequeathed them back to the estate before they both died. And Matthew Prichard, Christie's lucky young grandson to whom she gave away the play as a ninth birthday present before it opened, is still reaping the benefit.

St Martin's Theatre
West Street, London WC2N 9NZ
www.the-mousetrap.co.uk

# Wyndham's Theatre

Wyndham's Theatre, right by Leicester Square Tube station on the Charing Cross Road, is the only West End theatre with a bust of William Shakespeare on its exterior, a pleasing, symmetrical frontage of Portland stone. The bust is lodged in the central pediment of the principal elevation with three major bays, handsome windows, pilasters, balustrades and statuary all contained in a free classical style. In later life, the architect W.G.R. Sprague would design the delightful jewel box Edward VII theatre in Paris. His architectural Francophilia starts right here.

Even hard-bitten theatregoers catch their breath on entering the foyer, which exudes an air of pastel-coloured Gallic élan, a palpable sense of bouncing about among painted nymphs, shepherds and cherubs that could have been done by Boucher. The auditorium is no less gay and delightful, decorated in the style of Louis XVI, with the last surviving picture-frame proscenium in London, a floral design in the circular ceiling of pale blue and gold lit by a crystal chandelier. The two cantilevered curving balconies are rich in painted panels, and the boxes with bowed fronts are arranged on three storeys; the whole place is a model of elegance and a womb-like comfort and luxury.

In 1899, this was Sprague's first theatre – he had been articled to Frank Matcham for four years, and to Walter Emden for a further three – in an extraordinary run of designing six West End houses in as many years, and a love letter for his clients. The monograms entwined in plasterwork in the stalls – those of C.W. and M.M., Charles Wyndham and Mary Moore – proclaim not only one of the greatest West End love stories, and its consequent dynastic legacy, but signify, too, a theatre of special intimacy and romance. Even the boxes are tiny, with seating only for two. It's rumoured that the cosy balcony bar

*The most romantic theatre in London has intimate, bow-fronted boxes and an air of Gallic élan.*

was the first gay bar in London. Perhaps here's why: Sandy Wilson's coyly camp pastiche musical *The Boy Friend* ran here for six record-breaking years from 1954; Joe Orton's *Entertaining Mr Sloane*, with its street-wise male mascot in a white T-shirt causing sexual havoc in suburbia, opened in 1964; and Mart Crowley's hilarious *The Boys in the Band*, London's first explicit gay ensemble piece (though it came from New York), was a smash hit in 1969. But everyone who works here loves the place. And everyone who sees a play here loves it, too, absorbed by its seductive charms.

The actor-manager Charles Wyndham had run the Criterion since 1875, but dreamed of building a theatre of his own. In 1898, plans for a theatre on the current site faltered. The land belonged to the Marquis of Salisbury (the Prime Minister at the time) and he made it a condition of granting a green light that Wyndham, his favourite actor, was involved. The £10,000 cost was raised by Wyndham's mistress and leading lady at the Criterion, Mary Moore, twenty-five years his junior, through her society contacts. The lovers' affair,

dating from 1886, remained hush-hush for thirty years, as Wyndham's first wife did not die until 1916. He and Mary had just three years of marriage, Wyndham dying in 1919. From 1910, another great actor-manager, Gerald du Maurier (father of the novelist and playwright Daphne), was based in Wyndham's for fifteen years and, in 1926, Mary Moore leased the building to the American crime writer Edgar Wallace, who presented his own dramas over the next six years, including *On the Spot* (1930) starring Charles Laughton as the gangster Tony Perelli in one of his signature performances. Wallace lived above the shop, taking an apartment at the top of the theatre which is now modernised as comfortable, rather sleek, production offices and facilities.

Moore had been married to the somewhat dissolute playwright James Albery (who died in 1899) and had three sons with him, the second of whom, Bronson, took over the management of the Criterion, Wyndham's and New theatres from her (she died in 1931) in association with Charles's son, Howard. Howard Wyndham – not to be

*The old box office and doorways in the exuberant foyer.*

*The initials of Charles Wyndham are entwined elsewhere with those of his lover, Mary Moore.*

confused with the powerful Scottish producing company and pantomime purveyors, Howard & Wyndham – and Bronson Albery, especially, became prominent West End figures, as did Albery's son, Donald Albery, who succeeded him in management in 1932, and his grandson, Ian Albery, who also ran the family theatres before supervising the redesign of Sadler's Wells; Ian's younger brother, Tim, is an internationally renowned opera director.

The New Theatre on St Martin's Lane (renamed the Albery in 1973 and re-renamed the Noël Coward in 2006) is Sprague's twin creation, backing onto Wyndham's, and opening in 1903. Wyndham's itself teems with this interconnecting history – both venues are now owned by Delfont Mackintosh Theatres – while remaining an always fresh and attractive venue, not least on opening nights, when the centre aisle, an endangered species in the West End, alas, is restored in the front stalls and the lights dim on a new play. For many actors and stage and company managers, Wyndham's is a favourite house.

That sense of first night anticipation is heightened by a glance above the unique square proscenium, where an architrave supports two winged male angels holding oval portraits of Oliver Goldsmith and Richard Brinsley Sheridan, authors of the late-eighteenth-century comic masterpieces *She Stoops to Conquer* and *The School for Scandal*. Between them, an unidentified bust with golden wings is now thought to represent Mary Moore (which is only fair, as Charles Wyndham's bust is in the foyer). The festooned safety curtain, when it descends, depicts a much more Victorian angel in full flight, blowing on a slender bugle.

There's an evocative door from the green room to the off-stage area, which carries the names of acting luminaries down the years, and an external bridge crosses the alleyway, joining the fly floors of Wyndham's and the Noël Coward; this was constructed by Ian Albery in the mid-1970s as an economic and practical measure, creating a single stage door for both theatres, and a conduit of central heating pipes. But the bridge survives and occasionally serves as a two-way

*The ceiling of the auditorium, with Donald Albery's suspended chandelier.*

decoy escape route for a paparazzi-pursued mega-star – such as Madonna in *Up for Grabs* (2002) by David Williams in Wyndham's, or Daniel Radcliffe in *The Cripple of Inishmaan* (2013) by Martin McDonagh in the Noël Coward – keen to preserve both privacy and physical safety.

Radcliffe's appearance was part of a year-long tenancy of the Michael Grandage Company, a highly successful commercial adventure which, taken alongside more recent West End occupations by Jamie Lloyd's company at the Trafalgar Studios and Kenneth Branagh's at the Garrick, suggests a shift in producing patterns in the West End. But the post-war history of Wyndham's is already rich in milestone events: Graham Greene's first play, *The Living Room*, in 1953, Harold Pinter's *No Man's Land* starring Gielgud and Richardson in 1976 (a National Theatre transfer), Peter

Nichols' searing *Passion Play* in 1984, and two long runs – almost as long as *The Boy Friend*'s – of the musical *Godspell* in the 1970s and Yasmina Reza's *Art* (1996) translated from the French by Christopher Hampton, a clever three-hander about male friendship which thrived on the novel production ploy of changing an all-star cast every three months.

Donald Albery was a friend and admirer of the pioneering director Joan Littlewood and her Theatre Workshop at Stratford East. Following the run of *The Boy Friend*, he began a legendary four-year professional association during which he presented the West End transfers of *A Taste of Honey* and *The Hostage* (both in 1959), *Sparrers Can't Sing* (1961) and *Oh, What a Lovely War!* (1963). The period is memorialised in photographs and posters in the Littlewood bar, a cross-over room behind the grand circle. The royal circle bar has

*The fly floor, showing the use of hemp ropes.*

tributes to Jeremy Brett and Simon Cadell, popular actors associated with the theatre, while the downstairs stalls bar has a *Boy Friend* wall and etchings of the theatre in its opening weeks. Donald Albery had extended the family portfolio with a fourth theatre, the Piccadilly, in 1960, and sold on the group to Associated Newspapers in 1978, who retained Ian Albery as managing director. Ownership moved on again in 1984, with more upheavals and sales and the advent of the Ambassador Theatre Group and the departure of Ian Albery. The long lease on Wyndham's was finally acquired in 2005 by Cameron Mackintosh's DMT.

Mackintosh's first big West End hit had been the cabaret *Side by Side by Sondheim*, which moved to Wyndham's from the Garrick along the street in 1976. The connection is acknowledged in a painting by Francis Hamel, hanging in the foyer, of Sondheim's *Sunday in the Park with George* being watched in three-quarter profile by Mackintosh, like Alfred Hitchcock looming unexpectedly in one of his own films. This, and the sly addition of the initials C.M. to the front of the royal circle, were just two details in a major four-month refurbishment in 2008, which saw Sprague's original colour scheme of blues, creams and golds gloriously restored, new seats and an easy access box installed and the signature DMT two-toned striped wallpaper hung in the auditorium at every level. Even so, the place still really belongs to the canoodling ghosts of Charles Wyndham and Mary Moore.

Wyndham's Theatre

Charing Cross Road, London WC2N 0DA

www.wyndhamstheatre.co.uk

# Gielgud Theatre

The Globe on Shaftesbury Avenue was renamed the Gielgud in 1994 for two reasons: plans for a new Globe, Shakespeare's Globe, on Bankside were well advanced; and there was a growing lobby for naming a West End theatre in honour of its greatest twentieth-century star in the year of his ninetieth birthday. At an informal occasion to mark the rechristening, John Gielgud stood in the circular dress circle bar at the top of the double-height foyer and regaled the assembled colleagues and journalists of tales of triumph and disaster – disaster, mostly, he relished in his anecdotage – in this theatre. He had appeared, he recalled, in a 1928 comedy called *Holding Out the Apple* and had been obliged to utter the deathless line, 'I am holding out the apple, but you always give me the pip.' His pink, noble face creased with laughter, and he added through a mist of tears that the one consolatory pleasure for him in that rotten apple was the sight of his name up in lights for the first time ever: 'And now, when I walk along this Avenue that I love so much, there will at least be one name still on the marquee that I shall recognise.'

The theatre opened as the Hicks in 1906. The actor-manager Seymour Hicks had joined an ambitious venture of the estate agent Sydney Marler and the boot-maker Jack Jacobus to build two theatres and expand Jacobus's business at the same time. This was part of the building frenzy and speculation on the land that had been released with the opening of Shaftesbury Avenue in 1886, and the masterplan of the architect W.G.R. Sprague. The result was the Globe on the Rupert Street corner and (opening one year later) its matching partner, with a similar elevation, the Queen's on the Wardour Street side, with an enlarged boot and shoe emporium running across the frontage on Shaftesbury Avenue. When Hicks dropped out in 1909, the theatre was renamed the Globe.

*The handsome auditorium has a circular theme, pilasters and* putti *under a fine domed ceiling.*

*The sub-stage area, showing scenic bits and bobs, and a prop Corinthian pillar.*

*The star's dressing room backstage has a large bed, tall fridge and practical cupboards.*

That entrance foyer, a heart-lifting space of airiness in cream and gold, is similar at the upper level to the smoking gallery at the Aldwych, also by Sprague, and matched with another theatre on the same block, the Strand (now the Novello). The atmosphere is enhanced with pilasters and *putti* under the domed ceiling, leading to an auditorium that continues a circular theme. Brass rails, too, seem to run through the building like gleaming rivulets. The original décor in the two-tier theatre with a gallery behind the upper cantilevered circle was Louis XVI-style in Rose du Barri with ivory and gold enrichments; that scheme returned in a major 2007 refurbishment, panels of rose and grey-and-green striped wallpaper on a peach and dusky pink painted background ousting years of intervening red plush and velvet.

Between the wars, the Globe was a smart new writing address, operating for ten years under the management of the actress Marie Löhr and her husband, Anthony Prinsep, with plays by Somerset Maugham, A.A. Milne and Noël Coward and, from 1936, under the aegis of H.M. Tennent, the company named after its founder, Henry Moncrieff Tennent, whose protégé and junior partner, Hugh 'Binkie' Beaumont, assumed full control on Tennent's death in 1941. For over thirty years, this was indeed the epicentre of the West End, Gielgud appearing in fifteen plays – including a legendary 1939 all-star revival of *The Importance of Being Earnest*, which he also directed, with Edith Evans as Lady Bracknell, a performance immortalised in the 1951 movie – and producer Binkie ruling the roost with a fist of iron and a network of favourites. The Tennent offices

at the back of the upper circle were reached in 'the smallest lift in London' – room, just about, for two normal-sized people who didn't mind the look (or indeed, the smell) of each other too much – behind the box office (the shaft is now boarded up). Binkie's clientele were the pick of the box office stars: Gielgud in Christopher Fry, Coward and Graham Greene's *The Potting Shed*, Eileen Herlie in *Medea*, Paul Scofield in *A Man for All Seasons*, Maggie Smith and Kenneth Williams in a Peter Shaffer double bill and, in the post-Binkie era, between 1974 and 1998, no less than five Alan Ayckbourn titles, including his *Norman Conquests* trilogy (starring Tom Courtenay, Penelope Keith, Felicity Kendal and Richard Briers). The Globe opened as the Gielgud with, suitably enough, a new Hamlet, Stephen Dillane, directed by Peter Hall.

The lease on the theatre was taken by the powerful Prince Littler group in 1960. Forty years later, ownership passed to Andrew Lloyd Webber's Really Useful Theatre Group (and NatWest Equity, as private banking started to move into West End theatres) before Delfont Mackintosh acquired the whole island site in 2006, beginning a £20 million process of reinvention. The proposed communal foyer linking both theatres never materialised, and plans to build a new 500-seat Sondheim Theatre over the top of the site have been redirected towards the redesign of the Ambassadors, while the shoe shop, long departed, operated for a while as premises for Cecil Gee's men's outfitters. Mackintosh, who now owns the whole shebang, bought a Cecil Gee suit there for his first ever first night as a producer.

The free baroque style of the Gielgud's exterior remains

one of the most buoyant in London, with giant Ionic columns supporting a buttressed circular tower and dome, wonderful windows and balustrading. Inside, the 2007 refurbishment restored the boxes at the back of the dress circle as one big box, and the fine promenade, along transparent glass and curtains, remains, as does the lyrical plaster decoration of cherubs and musical instruments. There is new seating throughout and, as in most theatres these days, you are no more uncomfortable in the upper gallery (now the grand circle) than you are in the best stalls seats, and you all come through the same front door.

The dress circle bar, with a Gielgud bust and an amusingly truculent photograph of the great comedy actress Margaret Rutherford (Miss Prism in that 1939 *Importance*), is still one of the most breathtaking rooms in the West End, while the stalls bar is adorned with the affectionate show business caricatures of actor Clive Francis and a photograph of Andrew Lloyd Webber looking suspiciously like Lilian Baylis; this is, in fact, a portrait of the composer 'Beryl Waddle-Brown', who wrote the school anthem for a jolly hockey-sticks comedy, *Daisy Pulls It Off*, presented by her doppelganger at the Globe in 1983. The ghost of Binkie is remembered in a beautifully decorated and appointed small hospitality room just off the foyer; his famous offices are now occupied by the director Michael Grandage's producing company, a far less intimidating group than Binkie's clan. In the old anteroom by the top of the lift shaft, there's a framed telegram from Tennessee Williams complaining about cuts made to *A Streetcar Named Desire* (presented at the Aldwych in 1949). An air of glamour clings to the curved walls, even though this particular spot is now pressed into service as an office and changing room for front-of-house staff.

Gielgud Theatre

Shaftesbury Avenue, London W1D 6AR

www.gielgudtheatre.co.uk

*The double-height foyer atrium, showing the circular dress circle bar where John Gielgud accepted a nomination.*

# Phoenix Theatre

Willy Russell's Liverpool ballad musical *Blood Brothers* ran for twenty-one years at the Phoenix Theatre on Charing Cross Road. If you saw it when it first opened there in 1991, the distinctive glories of the venue would become a fading memory; to revisit two decades later was to rediscover a cavern of delights. Most London theatres are constructed on the site of a previous music hall or entertainment outlet. The Phoenix, built for the impresario Sidney Bernstein in 1930, arose in September of that year, three weeks after the Cambridge Theatre a few hundred yards away towards Covent Garden and five days before the Whitehall near Trafalgar Square, on the site of the rumbustious Alcazar, an open-all-hours talent show that later incorporated sideshows and slot machines.

The new Phoenix was aiming for something rather more sophisticated. It was designed by the trio of Giles Gilbert Scott (also responsible for Liverpool Cathedral and the red telephone box), Bertie Crewe and Cecil Masey, with Art Deco fittings, mirrored corridors and richly patterned ceilings by Theodore Komisarjevsky, the great Russian director and designer, and the second husband of Peggy Ashcroft, who played here in a season of *Twelfth Night* and Bulgakhov's *The White Guard* with Michael Redgrave in 1938.

It opened with Noël Coward's perennial comedy *Private Lives* starring the author, Gertrude Lawrence, Laurence Olivier and Adrianne Allen. In fact, this is much more the 'Noël Coward' theatre than the one on St Martin's Lane that now bears his name: Coward and Gertrude Lawrence called it 'our theatre' when they returned in 1936 with the short play/revue compilation *Tonight at 8.30*; Coward's Victorian comedy, *Quadrille*, written for the Lunts (the renowned transatlantic high comedy pairing of Alfred Lunt and Lynne Fontanne) played here in 1952, designed

*The auditorium.*

by Cecil Beaton; at a midnight matinée for Coward's seventieth birthday in 1969, the author entered the theatre on the stroke of midnight, having shortly before opened the bar that bears his name; and in 1973, the year of his death, the theatre hosted the first, and revelatory, West End revival of his 1939 'disgusting three-sided erotic hotchpotch' *Design For Living*, written for himself and the Lunts, in a production by Michael Blakemore starring Vanessa Redgrave, John Stride and Jeremy Brett.

The Noël Coward bar is now at dress circle level, a charmingly redecorated room with the signature Ambassador Theatre Group polished floorboards, the original Art Deco windows and a wonderful photographic celebration of the man known as the Master. This room is directly above the main entrance, and box office, on Phoenix Street. The other 'entrance' is around the corner on Charing Cross Road, where an elegant mini-rotunda decorated in duck egg blue (now repainted in cream) with fleur-de-lys ornamentation on classical pillars has the names of the architects engraved on its circular dome. Between these entrances, there is a block of apartments, rising above the ground-level shops, whose residents, during the 1970s, included the artist and filmmaker Derek Jarman, the extrovert actor Christopher Biggins and the colourful critic Jack Tinker; there were quite a few parties in celebratory honour of Noël and Gertie.

Recent refurbishments have revealed a marble floor, inlaid with brass strips, in the main foyer, reinforcing the temple-like, Italian villa atmosphere of the approach: there are two sets of heavy wooden doors, with striking metalwork above the inner set, and a coffered ceiling painted in red, green and gold. Phoenixes, griffins, flora, fauna and even a few fish abound everywhere in the plasterwork, an apt prelude to such remembered glories within as John Gielgud's Leontes and Benedick in the 1950s, Olivier and Vivien Leigh in Rattigan's *The Sleeping Prince* in Coronation Year, 1953, a four-play season of Hollywood stars in the mid-1970s – Rock Hudson, Lee Remick and Douglas Fairbanks Jr – Tom Stoppard's *Night and Day* (1978) starring Diana Rigg and John Thaw, and Martin Shaw giving his Elvis Presley in 1985. Either side of *Blood Brothers*, we had Irish revelry with Alec McCowen in Brian Friel's *Dancing at Lughnasa* and the extraordinary Dublin busker musical *Once*, audience mingling with band on the stage in a pre-show drink-up.

The ownership of the theatre has been wayward, moving from Sidney Bernstein to the powerful Prince Littler, then a property consortium before reverting to the family of the original owners, the Flint-Shipmans, who presided over the five-year tenure of Chaucer scholar Nevill Coghill's rude and raucous version of *The Canterbury Tales*. The theatre inside is squarer than most, with two perfectly proportioned circles. It has width, and is pleasingly shallow, and under ATG the auditorium is redecorated in red, with new carpeting, refurbished deco chandeliers and the preservation of such interesting oddities as random numbers in the wooden alcoves both in the stalls – each topped with a concave, shell-like deco fan – and on the dress circle walls, which seem to indicate the numbers of spectators ('three' or 'eighteen'), who might be accommodated in an overspill situation.

That cream and gold stalls corridor has a priceless display of posters, most of them from the all-powerful H.M. Tennent post-war producing era, with their distinctive red and black lettering. On the fly floor, high above the stage, there's a blackboard for the cues to be chalked for each show, but the current staff have preserved, as a memento, the board of cues for the second act of *Blood Brothers*, intending to preserve the chalk marks in perpetuity. There's not so much sentimentality attached to the orchestra pit, which is small and utilitarian. Undistinguished, too, are the neoclassical paintings around the top of the proscenium, mostly reclining nudes gathering dust and indifference. The glories remain lower down, mostly in the ornamentation but also the woodwork. Every time there's a circular room or feature, there's a curved wooden door, or rail, master carpentry in modest evidence. The finish of the place, in most of its aspects, is exquisite and detailed, an ideal setting for comedy from Coward to Stoppard, or literate musicals on a modest scale such as American imports *Two Gentlemen of Verona* (1973, with music by *Hair* composer Galt McDermot) or Stephen Sondheim's mordant retelling of interwoven fairy tales, *Into the Woods* (1990).

Phoenix Theatre
110 Charing Cross Road, London WC2H 0JP
www.phoenixtheatrelondon.co.uk

TOP *The cues for the second act of* Blood Brothers *preserved on the fly floor in perpetuity.*

ABOVE *The entrance to the stalls, a cream and gold corridor with mirrors and priceless posters.*

# Criterion Theatre

You enter most West End theatres at dress circle level and descend to the stalls. Nobs and toffs went straight from their carriages into their circle seats and bars without having to mix with hoi polloi in the pit or the paupers in the gallery. But the Criterion, built in 1873 on the site of a seventeenth-century coaching inn, and immediately adjacent to the statue of Eros in Piccadilly Circus, was the first completely underground, or basement, theatre in the capital, and this is because it was initially intended to be a concert hall.

It was part of an entertainment complex designed by Thomas Verity (who later designed the pavilion at Lord's Cricket Ground) for the caterers and wine merchants Spiers and Pond, which included, as well as the concert hall – which soon became a theatre – a restaurant, a pub and a gallery. The large, handsome frontage has separate, identical glazed canopied entrances (added in 1921) for the theatre and what is now a brasserie of fluctuating ownership and fortune. This brasserie is magnificently decorated with glittering, Byzantine mosaic strips, a large fireplace with marble columns at the far end suggesting the splendour of the original buffet area which served the theatre; it might, theoretically, one day revert to becoming the Criterion's own supper hall, though there are no signs of this happening very soon.

A grand east wing on the Regent Street side was demolished in the 1980s and replaced by a large modern office block which backs onto Jermyn Street and is bounded by Lilywhite's sportswear shop, McKinley financial services and an imposing fountain sculpture on the Haymarket angle of the rearing horses of Helios sculpted in 1992 by Rudy Weller. In that same year, producer Sally Greene and her trust refurbished the backstage area and

*The Criterion opened in 1874 as a concert hall, but this calm, stylish Beaux Arts auditorium, air-conditioned in 1884, was soon hosting theatre.*

*The ceiling above the box office in a foyer of mirrors and tiles which characterise the corridors and bars.*

reconfigured what is now called the Lord Attenborough stalls bar, a fine, L-shaped public space and a glamorous private party site. A feature of the Criterion public areas is the tiling, here done in the style of the St James and Jermyn Street quarter – as in Rowley's restaurant, for instance – and beautifully set off by the polished wooden counters and shelves (for drinks) and the stained-glass window back-lit by electricity.

Having opened in 1874, the Criterion was closed on fire safety grounds in 1882; air had to be pumped into the auditorium to minimise the risk of asphyxiation to the customers. It re-opened two years later as the first-ever air-conditioned theatre in London, with the original big grey metallic vents, still visible at the back of the stalls, rising through the building. On account of its subterranean status, there is no flying on the comparatively small stage (and little wing space), so the theatre also boasts the only London safety curtain to be operated on a roller blind. The auditorium is charming, simple, Beaux Arts style, with two circles (very good seats at the top) and cast-iron pillars supporting each circle that provide only minimally bad views of the stage; sight-lines in all theatres depend on how cleverly the designer has (or more usually hasn't) allowed for the architectural geometry. The flat circular ceiling has rococo relief panels, as does the seductive foyer with its fine wooden box office, mirrors, and yet more tiles. The Victorian and Edwardian scenery here would have been a basic fusion of painted cloths and standing 'flats'. The barer the design, the more effective the show, as demonstrated in two long-runners in recent years (each lasting nine years): the Reduced Shakespeare Company's satirical spoof of sketches and pratfalls and Patrick Barlow's ingenious 'physical theatre' send-up of *The Thirty-Nine Steps* by John Buchan.

The first manager was H.J. Byron, later a pantomime couplet specialist at Drury Lane, and he was succeeded by Charles Wyndham, who was the lessee until his death in 1919. In this period, Mary Moore was the leading lady in many comedies by the likes of Henry Arthur Jones; she married Wyndham in 1916, continued in charge until she herself died in 1931, when the theatre was carried on by her son, Bronson Albery, father of the manager and impresario Donald Albery and grandfather of producer Ian Albery. This great dynastic chain was the last of its kind in the modern theatre, comparable in some ways to the Stoll Moss empire, before the business of show became more corporately controlled and reliant on the backing of large private banks.

The Criterion exudes this sense of historical continuity as much as it revels in its own perfect proportions as a medium-sized playhouse, becoming virtually home to the great comedienne Marie Tempest in the late 1920s, hosting a famous *As You Like It* in 1936 with Edith Evans and a much younger Michael Redgrave (they became off-stage lovers, too) and, also starting in 1936, a three-year run of Terence Rattigan's first success, *French Without Tears*, starring Rex Harrison and Kay Hammond. Other long-runners have been Simon Gray's *Butley* (1971, starring Alan Bates), Alan Ayckbourn's *Absurd Person Singular* (1973) and Ray Cooney's *Run For Your Wife!* (1983, playing in excess of 1,600 performances).

There is access to Jermyn Street on one side of the upper circle, a surprising and very small dance floor installed as part of some licensing conditions and a smaller side bar now named after Sally Greene. The ornamental tiles in the extravagantly mirrored corridors alongside the stalls and circle are decorated with the names of classical composers from Handel, Verdi and Bellini through to Arne, Cimarosa and other forgotten nineteenth-century worthies. This tiling is being systematically restored by a company in Ironbridge, Staffordshire, in consultation with the original firm of tile-makers, Simpson's. A tradition of long runs means that the theatre is often available for events, showcases and drama school presentations in the day, though an attempt to launch a series of lunchtime conversations with critics proved as unpopular as some of the critics themselves. Theatre staff recall with a mixture of intense pleasure and sheer terror – what will he get up to next? – the last London appearance of the actor Nicol Williamson in his one-man show, *A Night on the Town*, a tribute to a fellow hell-raiser, John Barrymore, in 1994. The calm, rose-painted auditorium is in dramatic contrast to the tiles and Second Empire glories elsewhere, and a complete repaint, recarpet and reseat was accomplished a few years ago without once closing for business.

*This sculpture is known simply as 'The Lady Criterion'.*

Criterion Theatre
218–223 Picadilly, London W1V 9LB
www.criterion-theatre.co.uk

# Novello Theatre

The last great actor-manager Herbert Beerbohm Tree lived in the dome of the theatre he built, Her Majesty's, for twenty years; and crime writer Edgar Wallace took an apartment at the top of Wyndham's for several years in the 1930s. Ivor Novello, the extraordinarily popular composer of 'Keep the Home Fires Burning' and 'We'll Gather Lilacs' made an even more permanent and long-lasting home of a theatrical address; he moved into an apartment at the top of the Strand Theatre, with his mother, in 1913 and died there in 1951, aged fifty-eight. His funeral attracted crowds on the street comparable only to those subsequently of Winston Churchill and Princess Diana. So, how fleeting is fame? You feel as though the renaming of the theatre as the Novello in 2005, after a major refurbishment by Delfont Mackintosh Theatres, is a stern and long-overdue memory jog to the collective theatre-going consciousness.

Although Novello acted in many West End theatres, and his three major inter-war musicals – *Glamorous Night*, *Careless Rapture* and *The Dancing Years* – were presented at Drury Lane just around the corner, he acted only once at the Strand, and in the one play of his to be presented there, *Party*, in 1930, taking over the lead role in his signature 'first night' comedy as it transferred to the Gaiety across the road in the Aldwych. (That magnificent old musical theatre house closed in 1939, was bombed in the war and demolished in 1956.) The Strand was bombed in both wars, too, but Fred Terry, Gielgud's uncle, continued unfazed by a Zeppelin raid as the Scarlet Pimpernel on the first occasion and Donald Wolfit soldiered on in his lunchtime Shakespeare programme on the second.

The theatre was half of the third of W.G.R. Sprague's 'paired' projects following those of the Globe and the Queen's and the

*The Novello's triple-balconied auditorium was the last so constructed in London. The domed ceiling is left deliberately uncleaned. Mirrors and marble veneer add an opulent air.*

*The foyer is one of the most distinctive in the West End, with wrought-iron gates and banisters on a marble staircase.*

Wyndham's and the New, opening in May 1905 a few months before the Aldwych at the Drury Lane end of the block, the great Waldorf Hotel in between. The theatre was first named the Waldorf and was leased for twenty-one years to the powerful Broadway producing brothers, the Shuberts, but one of them, Sam, was killed in a railway accident (and is memorialised in the Novello) and their interest dissolved. In 1909, the theatre was briefly renamed the Strand until 1911 when an American producer, F.C. Whitney, took over and re-renamed it the Whitney. But that was another false start and, after a string of failures on the stage, the Strand was the Strand again in 1913 under the direction of Louis Meyer. The place got going seriously with light comedy in the era of the actor-manager Arthur Bourchier, the man who founded the OUDS in Oxford, co-lessee with his actress wife Kyrle Bellew from 1919 to 1927.

Sprague was no less brilliant at designing the Strand and the Aldwych on their respective corners than he had been with the Globe and the Queen's. Each has an elegant curved stone frontage and an exterior side wall of classical pillars, pediments and statuary both exuberant and imposing, though that of the Strand/Novello on Catherine Street is the finer, livelier and far cleaner. The Novello's foyer is something special, too: a vintage vestibule where the circle stairs are fitted out with black wrought-iron gates and banisters, guarded by two female figurines bearing lamps, in a rich setting of marble, mirrors and Georgian striped wallpaper.

The triple-balconied auditorium – the last in London, thanks to the insistence of the old London County Council – is decorated in gold, marble veneer and cream, with delicate floral wallpaper and the gold taps for fire hoses still visible in the stalls. The domed and painted ceiling in a heavily moulded surround has been left deliberately half-cleaned, for fear of damage; the obfuscation is caused by the exhalations of long-ago smoking patrons. Two boxes either side of the proscenium are not on the same level as the balconies and are framed by Ionic pilasters rising from large console brackets. The defining characteristic of this lovely theatre is the tympanum, bound by lintel and arch, over the proscenium, a startling bas-relief in tempered brass of an animated Apollo in a chariot drawn by four horses, attended by cupids and goddesses; it's the indoor games pay-off to the classical iconography on the exterior.

The refurbishment work has transformed the bars and public areas and decorated the royal box – which is virtually a stage box – and its retiring room with a portrait of Bourchier as Dr Johnson looming over the lavatory, a picture of Marry Jerrold and Lilian Braithwaite (a great friend of Ivor) in the long-running thriller *Arsenic and Old Lace* (1942) and a mini-shrine to Cyril Maude, who appeared at the Waldorf in between running the Haymarket and the Playhouse, which he opened. There are Novello portraits in both the royal box and the box facing, but the evocative production photographs are ranged primarily in the newly named Ivor's Bar at the back of the stalls, with its red striped wallpaper, polished wooden drinks shelves and one of the

Swedish artist Einar Nerman's incisive, elegant black and white cartoons of the composer whom he befriended when he worked here for *Tatler* in the 1920s. A curved alcove, the Whitney Room, has been decorated with a panoramic inset painting of the Lyceum, Strand, Gaiety and the Baroque church of St Mary le Strand.

The grand circle bar (in the middle tier) has been knocked right through to benefit from the central curve in the building and is now a beautiful room that can double as bar and meeting room, or small conference area, with large curving windows giving views on the Aldwych to left and right. Here, you can study not only photographs of Ivor's leading ladies – Mary Ellis, Olive Gilbert (who also lived here, in an apartment on the floor beneath Novello's), Dorothy Dickson, Elisabeth Welch – but also ashtrays, letters and other memorabilia from Redroofs, Ivor's country house for over twenty years in Maidenhead, Berkshire, now a theatre school where Kate Winslet was once head girl.

*The anteroom to the royal box, newly redecorated, a portrait of actor-manager Arthur Bourchier to the right.*

ABOVE *The tympanum above the proscenium, depicting Apollo in his chariot, a startling bas-relief in tempered brass.*
OPPOSITE *The view from the royal box. Like the boxes opposite, it is not aligned with the dress circle.*

The production history of the Novello is eclectic rather than significant, though Chekhov's *The Cherry Orchard*, the first great play of the twentieth century, was given its British premiere here in 1909. *Sailor Beware!* made Peggy Mount an unlikely star in 1955 and *No Sex Please, We're British* ran for eleven years from 1971, at first starring Michael Crawford, who used his gormless, acrobatic display to formulate the character of Frank Spencer in his television hit series *Some Mothers Do 'Ave 'Em* throughout the 1970s. Eleanora Duse played in the opening season of opera and plays in Italian. Musical long-runners of late include *Buddy: The Buddy Holly Story*, which ran here for six years (after running already for seven at the Victoria Palace) and *Mamma Mia!*, the Abba musical, which opened in 2012, on the most recent leg of its West End tour (starting at the Prince Edward, then the Prince of Wales).

Ivor died of a heart attack after returning home, having appeared in a performance of his own show, *King's Rhapsody*, at the Palace. The coffin, when it came, was too big to travel up to the flat in the tiny (now condemned and boarded-up) lift. So Ivor descended to ground level in a winding sheet and was tucked up in his last resting place in the foyer and thence transported to the funeral parlour. *And So To Bed* was the appropriate title of a 1926 play about the diarist Samuel Pepys, fitted out with new music and lyrics by Vivian Ellis, that opened here a few months later. 'Why is there always at least one tune in your plays that makes me cry buckets?' Novello had written to the musical comedy composer of *Mr Cinders* and *Bless the Bride*, whom he much admired, in 1949. This time, the tears were reciprocated.

Novello Theatre
Aldwych, WC2B 4LD
www.novellotheatrelondon.info

# Duke of York's Theatre

J.M. Barrie's Peter Pan first flew to Neverland in the Duke of York's in 1904. Eight years later on the same stage, a boy actor called Noël Coward made his West End debut as Slightly in *Peter Pan*; he was, said the critic Kenneth Tynan, 'wholly' in *Peter Pan* ever after. Several J.M. Barrie plays were premiered here under the innovative management of the American impresario Charles Frohman; Charlie Chaplin made his only stage appearance as an actor in London in 1905, as the boy Billy (he was fourteen years old) in William Gillette's *Sherlock Holmes*; Orson Welles directed, and appeared in, *Moby Dick* in 1955, and Alan Ayckbourn scored his first big hit with *Relatively Speaking* in 1967.

So this is a theatre suited to the subtlest inflections as well as heroic action. The intimate and the epic are equally at home in the Duke of York's. A theatre's productions seep into its architecture as much as they do the memories of audiences, and no modestly sized London house is held in more affection than Walter Emden's 1892 charming neoclassical venue, built for Frank Wyatt and his wife Violet Melnotte (known as 'Madame') on its own plot of land, back to back with the Garrick on Charing Cross Road, which Emden – who only designed eight theatres in all – had created with C.J. Phipps two years earlier.

The circle bar gives onto a small loggia overlooking St Martin's Lane, the proscenium is defined by stage boxes alone, a great dome decorated with acanthus, masks and winged figures creates a temple-like effect and, backstage, there's the last Strand Electric lighting machinery in the West End, out of use but too grand, and too ingrained, to budge. Under the stage there is a rickety ancient wooden structure, which lifted the *Peter Pan* pirates onto the *Jolly Roger* and Wendy aloft to her tree house, and a blocked off door to the rarely used orchestra pit. The whole place is so beguiling that when Mark Rylance appeared there in *Farinelli and the King* he

commissioned Stephen Reynolds, an executive of the parent company, Ambassador Theatre Group, to write him a history of the place.

First known as the Trafalgar Square Theatre, then the Trafalgar, the theatre became the Duke of York's in 1895. It was frequently flooded, as a tributary river ran underneath. Wyatt suggested they issue fishing rights instead of tickets at the box office. The attractive, classical cream-coloured frontage is on four storeys – the offices of producer Sonia Friedman occupy the top floor these days – the dressing rooms housed in a separate building at the back of the theatre at the end of an alley beyond one of two large iron gates either side of the theatre itself. Wyatt and Melnotte let the theatre on a long lease to Frohman in 1897. Two years later, Puccini saw an American one-act curtain-raiser here called *Madame Butterfly* and subsequently wrote the opera. Another event of historical significance was the mass meeting of actors here in December 1929, when they passed a resolution to form an actors' union, Equity. The meeting is commemorated with a plaque in the newly renovated circle bar, alongside a copy of the signatories to the resolution – Sybil Thorndike, Edith Evans, Irene Vanbrugh, Diana Wynyard among them – on a reproduction scroll; the original was kept for years under his bed by the former president of Equity, Marius Goring, but has now been returned to headquarters.

The stalls bar, recently redecorated, like the circle bar, in grey paint and polished floorboards, is named after J.M. Barrie and has a portrait of Nina Boucicault, the first Peter Pan, and other memorabilia on the walls. Frohman wrote the music for *Peter Pan* and presented the first ever West End ballet season, Anton Dolin and Alicia Markova playing a ten-week season in 1935. The theatre was damaged during the Blitz and was closed for three years from 1940. Redecoration under new ownership was undertaken in 1950 when Cecil Beaton designed a box office (now stored at the Victoria & Albert Museum) and a retiring room behind the royal box. That retiring room was the scene of the best-documented appearance of the ghost of Violet Melnotte in the mid-1960s. Violet's grandmother used to clean the theatre – it was very much a family affair – and 170 years on so did the grandmother of a woman called Judy Murphy who, as a girl, was left by her grandma in the retiring room with a bag of crisps while she continued cleaning elsewhere. A lady

*The last Strand Electric lighting machinery in the West End, out of use but immoveable.*

*A copy of the 1929 signed agreement to form the actors' union Equity.*

*The below-stage apparatus that allowed Peter Pan to fly in the 1904 production.*

with a long dress and train and wearing a tiara appeared in the room and asked Judy what she was doing. 'I'm eating crisps.' 'Well, that's all right, isn't it?' said the ghost and walked past Judy into the box. Judy's grandma came in just in time to see the ghost's train disappear round the corner. 'Who was that?' she asked Judy. 'The Queen.' There was nobody in the box, nor anyone else in the theatre.

Major alterations to the auditorium were made when Capital Radio acquired the theatre in 1980. They restored the original decorative colour scheme of cream, gold and russet, installed a recording studio on the top floor and gallery – the gallery remains out of use – and removed a forest of pillars in the stalls beneath the circle, thereby improving the sight-lines; the circle was then sustained by two cantilevered beams under the upper circle.

The Royal Court took over the theatre while their own home in Sloane Square was refurbished during the 1990s, and developed a broken-down look to the place, painting the interior walls black. Since then, owners ATG have extensively redecorated – not only the bars, but also the interior, with plum-coloured seating and velveteen finishing – and have restored the fittings, repainted the auditorium a calming matt blue and rechristened a modernised and darkened royal retiring room as an all-purpose lounge facility for VIP patrons with a distinct 'club' vibe. The golden sofa and lush swag of Beaton's design are echoed in the furnishings in the circle bar, which also has its own 'retiring' area at the far end, as well as access to the loggia and a view of the street. When not too crowded, this remains one of the most delightful small rooms in London theatre. Outside, the lower half of the first-storey frontage is currently painted black, with two small topiary trees in boxes standing sentry-like in the entrance to the pinkish square foyer, the whole place guarded by the huge iron gates, one of which retains an original Victorian street lantern.

Duke of York's Theatre

St Martin's Lane, London WC2N 4BG

www.dukeofyorkstheatre.com

# Savoy Theatre

There are two reminders in the Savoy Court, where taxis line up and drive on the right-hand side to the front of the hotel, of the history of this pocket of land in medieval times: a golden crusader standing astride the great silver stainless-steel detached pediment to the hotel; and, to the right of the entrance to the adjacent theatre, a wall plaque declaring that the palace of the Savoy – on a site first granted to the Earl of Savoy and Richmond by Henry III – was burned and destroyed by rebels led by Wat Tyler in 1381.

Almost exactly 500 years later, on 10 October 1881, the impresario Richard D'Oyly Carte opened his Savoy Theatre on that same site between the Strand and the Embankment and, three years later, with the profits accruing to his sensationally successful collaboration with Gilbert and Sullivan, whose *Patience* had opened the theatre and heralded their decade of Savoy Operas, D'Oyly Carte built the Savoy Hotel among the ruins of the old palace. It's an incredible story, and that of the Savoy Theatre has continued to be one of destruction and renewal: a brand new masterpiece of an Art Deco theatre in 1929 which was destroyed by fire in 1990 and re-opened, fully restored to its original glory, three years later.

The fire was an act of arson, but no one was charged, the insurance was paid and the case long since closed. The manager of the Savoy at the time was hoping the destruction of the Art Deco interior might prompt a more fit-for-purpose, modern replacement, but the terms of the insurance authorised only an exact 'reinstatement' of the theatre's original 1929 identity. None of the stage or backstage was affected, as the iron safety curtain was 'in' at the time of the fire in the small hours of 12 February 1990. Still, when the theatre re-opened, gleaming with jazz age

*The fully restored 1929 Art Deco interior, with silver coffered panelling either side of the stage.*

silver foil, mirrors and seats in five colours (three shades of red, plus yellow and green), it had a new flying system, an enlarged orchestra pit and updated lighting and technology. It was, and remains, a marvel, a sight for sore eyes.

D'Oyly Carte was immensely proud of the 1881 theatre designed for him by C.J. Phipps, with the main entrance around the back on Savoy Lane (formerly Somerset Street). And he was proud because this was the first public building in the world to be fully illuminated by electricity. The experiment might have failed – he kept the pilot light of the central sunburner fully alight in case it did – but this innovation signalled the end of foul odours from the oxygen-consuming gas burners. There was another social side effect: diamonds sparkled so effectively in the improved lighting that coloured stones went out of fashion; garish maquillage was out, too, as ladies discovered that the new illuminated density made them resemble harlots unless they softened their make-up. D'Oyly Carte also encouraged a new simplicity in the auditorium, which did away with cherubs and mythological deities in favour of delicate plaster modelling, colours of white, pale yellow and gold and 'blue plush of an inky hue' (his words) in the stalls, with seats of stamped velvet in the balcony and curtains of yellowish silk, 'brocaded with a pattern of decorative flowers in broken colours'.

This, then, was the setting for the premieres of six Gilbert and Sullivan satirical and musical masterpieces: *Iolanthe*, *Princess Ida*, *The Mikado*, *Ruddigore*, *The Yeomen of the Guard*, and *The Gondoliers*. There followed in the new century important seasons of Bernard Shaw and Shakespeare under the management of Harley Granville Barker until,

after the premiere of R.C. Sherriff's great First World War play *Journey's End* in 1929, the three-tier auditorium was completely rebuilt (in five months) by architect Frank A. Tugwell, with interior design by Basil Ionides, within the existing structure, the entrance finally settled (after moving back and forth) in Savoy Court to match and conform to the Art Deco frontage of the hotel.

The novelist Arnold Bennett hailed the most beautiful theatre in London (outside of Covent Garden) and audiences spoke of a modern miracle in the daring, Modernist and indeed Futurist characteristics of what Ionides had done. There were metal curtains for windows, brass rams for door handles, two lofty walls of silver and gold fluting – craftily disguised ventilation shafts – clusters of embossed green balloons on stippled orange wallpaper in the dress circle bar, a gorgeous double-windowed box office, fountains and figurines and Moroccan green leather doors, with brass studs, throughout every bar and public area in the building. The seating colour scheme on three levels (just two circles) was exactly replicated on the house tabs onstage. And there was just one box, to the right of the auditorium, which serves as a royal box when required, but which became almost a second home for Winston Churchill in the 1950s.

That box floats on the front wall of the auditorium which, on both sides, is a floor-to-ceiling sheet of silver coffered Chinese-designed panelling, every panel different, every one stuffed with animal and human figures, or flora and fauna, or just jazzy sculptured shapes. It's a contained riot of pictorial pleasure, slightly contaminated in the 1950s when redecorated in a dusty gold, but restored to shining silvery style in 1993, and treated to a silver-leaf upgrade in

2013. That latter update also benefited one of the unsung areas of the theatre, the upper circle bar, which has daylight, some lovely angular lines and one of the several monkey relief silver panels dotted throughout the place. The first theatre's foyer is a reception area with a charming Egyptian urn fountain with bare-breasted attendants; but this is a replica piece, as the original was looted on the night of the 1990 fire.

On that night, the theatre's popular chairman, Hugh Wontner, was first to the scene of devastation in the Strand. Soon joined by his theatre manager, Julian Courtenay, he roamed the rubble for a couple of hours, unable to touch the red hot handrails, or see through the smoke and the moisture in the atmosphere from the fire hoses. Sir Hugh was a hotelier and politician who was chairman, and then president, of the Savoy hotel group in a direct line from D'Oyly Carte's empire. He was grievously upset but turned to Courtenay at 5 a.m. and said, simply, 'Well, your job's going to change. The theatre has to be rebuilt.' And so it was, though Sir Hugh never lived to see it. He died towards the end of 1992. When the redecoration was nearly complete, his likeness was subtly included as a sort of stencil right at the top of the ceiling which was, once again, as it had been in 1929, a blue and white summer sky, from the proscenium arch to the back of the upper circle. After a celebratory dance programme re-opening the theatre, the first play was a revival of Noël Coward's *Relative Values*, which had received its premiere at the Savoy in 1951. Margaret Courtenay, Julian's mother, was in the new cast, and secured the few laughs that were on offer. The play had dated even as the theatre itself was reborn.

Savoy Theatre

Strand, London WC2R 0ET

www.savoytheatre.org

*Each seat in the Savoy is of a different colour: three shades of red as well as yellow and green.*

*Stage door lantern found under the stage, Duke of York's Theatre.*

# Index

# Acknowledgements

I would like to thank Nick Allott and William Differ at Delfont Mackintosh Theatres; Adam Speers and Stephen Reynolds at Ambassador Theatre Group; Mark Fox at the Really Useful Theatre Group; Nica Burns and Anna Charles at Nimax Theatres; David Lan and Charlotte Bayley at the Young Vic; Murray Melvin at Theatre Royal Stratford East; Ned Seago at the Old Vic; Susie McKenna at the Hackney Empire; Claudia Conway at Shakespeare's Globe; Arnold Crook at the Theatre Royal, Haymarket; Steve Tompkins (Haworth Tompkins); all the house managers and backstage staff who made us welcome; and Ian Albery, Howard Jepson, Nick Bromley, John Earl, Iain Mackintosh and Richard Pilbrow. – MC

This book is dedicated to my parents William and Freda Dazeley MBE, and to my family – Jannith, Tiger and Indigo. I would like to thank them for all their encouragement; Michael Coveney for his fantastic contribution and insight; agent and producer Sarah Ryder Richardson; digital manager Esther Salmon; my publisher Andrew Dunn for inspiring the project; editor Michael Brunström and designer Sarah Allberrey at Frances Lincoln for their invaluable expertise. Finally, enormous thanks to all the theatres and their management, for their support and generosity in allowing me access. – PD

Brimming with creative inspiration, how-to projects and useful information to enrich your everyday life, Quarto Knows is a favourite destination for those pursing their interests and passions. Visit our site and dig deeper with our books into your area of interest: Quarto Creates, Quarto Cooks, Quarto Homes, Quarto Lives, Quarto Drives, Quarto Explores, Quarto Gifts, or Quarto Kids.

*London Theatres*
Copyright © 2017 Quarto Publishing plc
Text copyright © 2017 Michael Coveney
Photographs copyright © 2017 Peter Dazeley
Foreword copyright © 2017 Mark Rylance

First published in 2017 by Frances Lincoln Ltd,
an imprint of The Quarto Group.
The Old Brewery, 6 Blundell Street,
London N7 9BH, United Kingdom
T (0)20 7700 6700   F (0)20 7700 8066
www.QuartoKnows.com

A catalogue record for this book is available from the British Library.

978-0-7112-3861-9

Printed and bound in China
9 8 7 6 5 4 3 2 1